AN UNNATURAL DEATH

The Frank May Chronicles

Lawrence Friedman

A QP Mystery

QP Books
New Orleans, Louisiana

AN UNNATURAL DEATH

The Frank May Chronicles

A QP Mystery, published in 2012 by QP Books.

QUID PRO, LLC
5860 Citrus Blvd., Suite D-101
New Orleans, Louisiana 70123
www.qpbooks.com

ISBN 978-1-61027-131-8 (pbk)
ISBN 978-1-61027-132-5 (ePub)

Printed in the United States of America.

Publisher's Cataloging-in-Publication

Friedman, Lawrence.
    An unnatural death / Lawrence Friedman.
        p. cm.
    Series: *The Frank May Chronicles* (#4)
    ISBN/EAN 978-1-61027-131-8
1. Lawyers—California—Fiction. 2. San Mateo (Cal.)—Fiction. 3. May, Frank (Fictitious character)—Fiction. I. Friedman, Lawrence. II. Title. III. Series.
PS3557.F811N45 2012   814.'3'553—dc22
                                          2012019476

for Leah, Jane, Amy, Sarah,
David, Lucy, and Irene

AN
UNNATURAL
DEATH

1

"I think somebody murdered my aunt."

That was the kind of sentence that was bound to catch a person's attention. It certainly caught mine. I looked over my desk at Barbara Homans. Was she joking? I found this hard to believe. She wasn't the sort of woman who told jokes. Anyway, I had never noticed much of a sense of humor. She was, in fact, a rather serious person. I had known Barbara for a number of years. She was a woman of a certain age—fifty, I would guess. Nice-looking, dignified. Divorced, no children. Dressed in solid good taste.

She had worked for years, some kind of administrative job, a company that made software; exactly what, I have no idea. The job paid well, but, more important, in some of the early years, right after it was founded, she picked up a bundle of stock. The company grew and grew; so that when she decided to quit the job, she was worth a fair amount of money. She had family money, too. This family money figures in this story; the software stock does not.

Anyway, Barbara was one of my clients, and she, no doubt, considered me "her lawyer."

"You can't mean that," I said to her. "The kind of people we know don't murder each other."

"Frank, I meant every word."

"Somebody murdered Aunt Harriet? I mean, how can you say that? She was an old lady, Barbara. She was over 80... 83, wasn't she? She had arthritis.... Well, that doesn't kill you. But... she died a natural death; you told me that yourself."

She looked at me with a kind of impatience. "Of course I said that, Frank. What else was I going to say? It looked that way. I mean, it seemed very natural. All I had to go on were suspicions."

"She died in her sleep, didn't she?"

"She died in bed, yes. She died at night, yes. But I think somebody smothered her with a pillow. Isn't that the way people do it?"

I had no idea how people do it. I never smothered anybody with a pillow. I don't know people who smother people with pillows. I've seen that sort of thing in the movies; or on TV. But I have no personal experience with smothering; I use a pillow myself, every night, like most people. But I don't think of a pillow as a murder weapon.

"It's easy, isn't it?" she said.

"What's easy?"

"Smothering somebody. With a pillow."

"Barbara, how would I know? You think I kill people with pillows? I don't kill people at all! I'll admit, I'm tempted with some of my clients. Not you, naturally. But, believe me, I never acted on these impulses. The Bar Association doesn't like it if you commit murder. And I would never murder a client; that I can tell you. I need their business."

"You're not taking me seriously," she said.

She was right about that, so I apologized. "I can see you're upset. I'm sorry if I seem callous. It's just that... Barbara, I can't believe you're actually saying these things."

"I can't believe it myself. But I had to tell *somebody*, Frank. It's been eating away at me."

I leaned back in my chair. It was a hot day, in the middle of summer. It was late afternoon, when it's often as hot as it gets in summer in California, and it was fairly stuffy in my office. The air conditioning didn't seem to be working. I made a mental note to call somebody connected with the building and enter a complaint. I was sweating, and I had an irresistible urge to loosen my collar.

Barbara seemed not to notice how hot it was in the room; or to take notice of anything else. She had a look on her face of... well, let's call it deadly earnestness. And the way she gripped her purse—it was a *serious* grip, if you know what I mean. I hated the direction this conversation was going. We had other things to talk about and this was an interruption. But I had to pursue the matter, at least for the time being, if only to mollify her. I said, "Barbara, what's the basis for all this? You said you had suspicions. Suspicions of what?"

"I know somebody wanted to kill Aunt Harriet. She practically told me so herself."

"She *told* you?"

"Well, not exactly. She said, Barbara, I have something that's preying on my mind. Those were her words. Then she, well, she didn't tell me very much. She was, I guess you'd say, somewhat cryptic. But that's what I think she meant. She meant somebody was threatening her. Frank, I think she was actually afraid."

"When did this happen, this conversation?"

"About a week before she died."

Until the point when Barbara blurted out her comment, about somebody killing her aunt, we had had a routine session. Boring even. But I should say something about where this was all taking place. The two of us were sitting in my office, in San Mateo, California. My law office. I'm a lawyer. I should tell you that before we go any further. My name is Frank May. I'll give you more of the details later. Barbara was Barbara Homans. She was my client—I think I mentioned those two facts.

Not that she normally needed a lawyer. What brought us together, right now, was Aunt Harriet's estate. Aunt Harriet was Harriet Wingate. She was in her 80's, as I said, and had recently passed on. Aunt Harriet had been more or less married (I'll explain that later), but apparently had no living descendants. At least we didn't think so. More about *that* later too.

The family situation was this: Harriet was the last survivor of her siblings. There was a whole flock of nieces and nephews; but they lived somewhere else, some of them even in Australia, which is about as far away as you can get. Barbara along with her sister Karen were the ones that mattered most to Aunt Harriet. They were the only nieces who lived in the

Bay Area. Their own mother, Harriet's sister Ruth, had died of breast cancer some twenty years earlier, and ever since then these two women had been close to their aunt. She was, I guess, a kind of substitute mother for them. She and Barbara were very fond of each other.

Karen's last name was Bridges. She was 50-something, and she was a widow. I know nothing about the late Mr. Bridges. I think he died quite young. The marriage had produced a daughter, whose name escapes me. Anyway, this daughter was married to a dentist and was living in Cleveland, Ohio, with her husband and I think some children. She has absolutely no part to play in this story, so you can forget about her, if you wish.

Aunt Harriet had died early in August. The conversation with Barbara, the one I'm telling you about, took place more or less on a Friday toward the end of August, give or take a day or two. I don't remember the exact date. I could look it up, but the precise day doesn't matter.

My first impression, to be sure, was that the whole idea, about somebody murdering Aunt Harriet, was completely absurd. But Barbara seemed quite serious. I felt I had to go along with her so I asked, "What exactly did she say, Barbara? When you had that conversation, you know, the one where you felt she was, uh, in danger. You haven't told me the facts."

"I'll give you the whole story, Frank. But first, I want to back up a bit, and fill you in on some aspects of our situation. My aunt—well, I don't want to say she had changed in recent months; but in a way, she was different; she seemed worried, preoccupied. Oh, she tried to hide it, but I could tell... she had something on her mind."

"And she didn't tell you what it was."

"No, she didn't. Maybe it would be more accurate to say she *wouldn't*. I spoke to her about it, several times. I said, Harriet, what's on your mind? You seem so... troubled."

"And what did she say?"

"Nothing. She changed the subject. But once, we were having dinner together, oh, maybe a month or so before she died, she did open up a little bit. She said something, well, it sounded very strange to me. She said: Barbara, I've done some terrible things in my life. I said, I can't believe that, Aunt Harriet. You're a wonderful, wise, loving person. She said, maybe I am now, thank you for saying that, but I wasn't always. I made... mistakes. I said, do you want to tell me about them? What I meant, Frank—I didn't want to pry; but I thought, she's bothered by something, and maybe it would help, you know, if she talked about it. But she said, no, she'd rather not."

"You got nothing more out of her?"

"Only this: she repeated that she had done some terrible things, and she said, I'm paying for it now. She said it again: I'm paying for what I did, Barbara; and in some ways, I'm willing to make up for my wrongs. But the price is going up, and I don't know if I can do it anymore."

"What did you say?"

"I told her I loved her, and I wanted to help her, and if she was in any kind of trouble, she could call on me, and please do that, and I said, this is very mysterious, I have no idea what you're talking about, and I said, you know, Aunt Harriet, you can tell me *anything*, you can trust me, I repeated that; but she just smiled and said, well, maybe when the time comes; and that was that."

"And you have no idea what she was referring to?"

"None at all," Barbara said. "And then: well, then came this other business. It was, I think, a Saturday night. I'm sure it was. I took her to the movies. I don't remember what we saw. Some comedy. Aunt Harriet didn't mind sex in the movies, but she didn't like violence. I picked her up, we had a quick bite in a Chinese restaurant, then we went to the movies. Aunt Harriet seemed very quiet—not at all like her usual self. She was quite a character. Well, you remember; you knew her, Frank. We had coffee after the movie, in Palo Alto, on University Avenue. One of those cafes. Usually she wanted to go right home, go to bed. She wasn't a night person. But she said, let's get some coffee, Barbara, I want to talk to you. Her mood was... funny, you know—distant, sort of. It was like that other time. I said, Harriet, now I'm sure of it, there's something on your mind. She said, yes there is. So we went for the coffee.

"And so there we were, sitting and drinking our coffee, and I waited for her to talk. But then she seemed to change her mind, said she didn't want to talk about it after all. I was getting worried. I said, is it your health, Aunt Harriet? She said: well, no. Not exactly. I asked her, is it connected with that other thing, the thing you mentioned, you know, when you told me you made some mistakes. She said, well, yes, it is. Then she said something terrifically odd."

"What was that?"

"She said 'if something happens to me...' but then she broke off the sentence. I said, what do you mean, what's going to happen to you, you're not telling me something—have you been to the doctor, I know that something's wrong. I remembered, I had gone with her, to the doctor—I mean, I dropped her off there, the week before, and picked her up, at the clinic, you know? The Palo Alto Clinic. That's where she went, for checkups and things. I thought, maybe she got bad news. From lab tests, maybe. But she said, oh, no, it's nothing like that, but.... Then she wouldn't say any more for a while. Just stirred her coffee with a spoon. It was very strange. I told her she *had* to confide in me, she just had to. Finally she said, I don't know if I ought to tell you. You see, I'm... pretty frightened. Or words to that effect. Of course I was startled, I asked her, frightened? Yes, she said, I'm really afraid. Afraid of what? Of somebody? Is somebody trying to hurt you?"

"Why did you ask her that? What made you think somebody wanted to hurt her?"

"Well, Frank, I had a reason. Because of something that happened a while before that...."

"Something that happened? What?"

"Actually, more than one thing. The first was... well, let's skip that part for now. I'll tell you some other time. Maybe. The other thing was this. About a week before she died, and just before this conversation, I was driving by, and decided to drop in and see her. I used to do that a lot. Well, to my surprise, there was a police car parked out in front. I got quite scared. What were the police doing there?

"Naturally, I was alarmed. I thought, my God, something's happened, something's wrong. So I rushed inside, and there was Aunt Harriet, talking to some policemen, two of them I think. They were all sitting in the living room. She looked extremely nervous. I said, 'Aunt Harriet, what's the problem?' She said, 'never mind.' She said to the policemen, this is my niece. They seemed to be just about through, with whatever it was they were doing. They got up and left the house. I said, 'Aunt Harriet, you've got to tell me what this is all about. Why were those policemen here?' But she absolutely wouldn't say."

"And... you still don't know?"

"Not a clue. Still: you can imagine my reaction... when she made this other comment. I tried to get her to say more, but she said I would have to wait. She said, yes, she was afraid of somebody, somebody wanted to harm her, those were her very words. She said maybe she would tell me later. I was very alarmed. I said, if you mean what you're saying, Harriet, then we should do something."

"And what did she say?"

"She said, no, not now; maybe later."

"And you don't know what she was referring to?"

"I had a vague idea. I don't want to share it with you, though—at least not yet, Frank... not until I know more, OK? Anyway: I said, we have to go to the police. But she laughed. She said, that wouldn't do any good. I was sorry I mentioned the police, because it flashed into my mind, the police were *already* involved, somehow.... I probed a bit; but Aunt Harriet was a stubborn woman, and she changed the subject. A week later she was dead."

"It could be a coincidence, Barbara. Her dying, I mean. She could have had a heart attack. Old people do, after all."

"Yes... but still, she was very healthy. I know she was old. But I talked to her doctor yesterday. I asked him point blank what he thought about Aunt Harriet dying, her health, and so on. He admitted he was surprised when he got the news. You see, he was away at the time. He was on vacation, and he found out she was dead when he came back. That was his word: surprised. I asked him why. She seemed in such good shape, he said, for her age. But then he said, well, after all, she *was* 83 or 84, he didn't remember her exact age; and sometimes these things come on all of a sudden."

"That's very true," I said, "take my grandmother—"

But Barbara was not about to take my grandmother. She plunged ahead: "So, all in all, it was very suspicious, don't you think? And this business with the will.... You have to admit, Frank, there's something fishy going on."

Yes, I had to admit it. Aunt Harriet, as I said, had been a client of mine. I drew up her Last Will and Testament. Or what I thought was her Last Will and Testament.

It was an easy and straightforward will. Aunt Harriet was quite a rich woman. A very rich woman, in fact. She inherited money from her husband, Joseph Wingate, who died about twenty years before her. Joseph Wingate had been a businessman, and a very successful one; and when he died, he left everything to his widow. Harriet was shrewd and careful; she made sure that the money kept growing. She lived modestly, for a woman of her wealth—not that she scrimped and saved, but she lived within her very ample means.

Joseph, for example, had left her some real estate in Silicon Valley and the very large house the two of them shared. She sold the house at an enormous profit and bought a smaller house, where she lived until she died. She kept the rest of the real estate, and sold it off gradually, always for enormous profits.

Well, part of this was luck. Everybody wants to live in Silicon Valley or anywhere around the San Francisco area. Can you blame them? No ice and snow; and in summer, no mosquitoes and no humidity. No wonder people flock to northern California. I'm so lucky I bought my house a long time ago. Today, you just can't touch a house in the Bay Area; they're astronomically expensive. The most modest sort of bungalow is a fortune. We have too many millionaires and billionaires around. I mean, money that would buy a mansion in Buffalo or Fargo wouldn't get you a mobile home in a trailer park out here. And while the real estate market was booming, even an idiot could make money out of real estate. And Harriet Wingate was no idiot. She knew when to buy and when to sell.

In addition, she had a nice portfolio of stocks and bonds; and she paid close attention to the market. Her investments had grown to many millions of dollars. I think twenty million, at least. We won't know for sure until we prepare an inventory.

The will. Yes. Nothing startling. She left money to a few charities, and small gifts to some of her friends; also a few thousand dollars to each of her far-off nieces and nephews. The rest of it, the bulk of the estate, went one-half to her husband Tommy, and one quarter each to her two favorite nieces, Barbara and Karen.

She named Barbara executor. If Barbara died or resigned, Karen would take over. Apparently Tommy, whatever his talents, was not her idea of someone she wanted to manage her estate.

Quite a straightforward will, in other words. Nothing fancy. The only oddity *was* the money she left to her husband, Tommy. Of course, there's nothing unusual about leaving half your money to your spouse. It's quite normal. What wasn't normal was this particular spouse. I don't mean to imply anything was wrong with Tommy—for now, I'll just mention that Tommy was 23 years old. Not a day older. Harriet Wingate, you will remember, was in her 80's. At least sixty years difference. That's a lot, if you ask me. In other words, they were not your ordinary married couple. They were June and December. He was June.

June and December does happen. But usually it's the other way around. Rich old goats marry trophy wives. Rich old ladies, for the most part, have more sense.

Right now, there was an even greater problem with the will: nobody could find it. It had vanished into thin air. Barbara looked; Karen looked; other people looked. Not a trace of it.

I was the one who prepared the will. Harriet Wingate was my client—had been for years. Not that I ever did much for her. I forget who recommended me to her. Mostly, I wrote her wills. This was a new will, but it wasn't much different from the one before it. She changed some of the smaller gifts, and she added a bit for the nieces and nephews, even the ones in Australia. She also added a friend or two, and dropped a few, including an old friend named Hilda. Harriet told me, it was because of Hilda's daughter's wedding. Hilda told her they were inviting 500 people. And it was a second marriage! "I said to Hilda, this is disgusting, you're spending a fortune. And the actual wedding, it was so vulgar, they had this loud music, some rock and roll band, the noise could wake the dead. And the bride was so drunk she could hardly stand up. I told Hilda I found the whole thing repulsive, and she laughed and said, it's the way things are these days. Well, I thought, if she's throwing her money around like that, she doesn't need mine." And that was the end of Hilda's modest legacy.

She also dropped a charity here, added a charity there. "That fund for people with diabetes," she said to me, "I used to like them, Joseph had diabetes, did you know that? But they keep sending me things, calendars, shopping bags, it's like Hilda, they're just wasting money on that junk; I'm not leaving them a cent." She switched to Parkinson's disease and kidney dialysis.

Harriet had strong ideas about everything. She left a few thousand dollars to Edna her cleaning lady, and to a delivery boy who brought her groceries; she didn't even know his name, I had to call Safeway to find out. He works hard, she said, and he always calls me ma'am. He'll amount to something some day.

I took the instructions, wrote the will (it wasn't much work), and Harriet came to my office to sign it. She seemed perfectly normal to me. She was dressed in a plain black dress, with a bright yellow belt. She wore a strand of pearls. Celia, my wife, could tell you more about what she was wearing. I'm tone deaf when it comes to women's fashions, if you know what I mean.

Harriet seated herself, we exchanged some small talk, and then we got down to business. I showed her the will, I explained what was in it, I read her the relevant parts, I skipped over the dull technical things, and made it all as clear as I could. She nodded her head. I asked her if this was what she wanted. She said yes. She was ready and willing to sign.

I needed two witnesses. My practice was to call in two young lawyers, young women, associates at a firm in the next building. I'm a solo practitioner, I don't have partners. The head of the firm next door was an old friend of mine, Richie Stern. He does shopping centers and condominiums. We don't compete, and he's happy to lend his associates, when we need witnesses for wills.

The whole thing went smoothly—why not? It always goes smoothly. There's no magic to it; it's completely routine. Harriet signed, the two young lawyers added their names as witnesses, and that was that.

When we were finished, I thanked the witnesses, Sonia and Andrea, offered them coffee, which they refused, and we said goodbye. I smiled at Harriet Wingate. I always worry about elderly clients who come in to sign their wills. I don't want them to think about dying. It's too morbid.

"You'll live twenty more years," I said to her. "We'll have dozens more wills, Harriet. I promise you."

She said: "You're a liar, Frank. Dozens more? I'm 83. But... well, you're a good man. And I'm glad we've got this over and done with."

"And the old will? Be sure to destroy it, won't you?"

She nodded. Then I told Aunt Harriet it would be best if I kept the original will, put it in my vault. That's where I keep my clients' wills, if they let me. I never liked the fact that she had always kept her wills in her home. Houses aren't safe places for wills. "Really, Harriet," I said. "Leave it with me, the will. I do this all the time. It's... pretty standard."

But Aunt Harriet refused. She said she wanted it where she could look at it—she'd put it in a drawer, and not to worry.

"You can look at a xerox," I said. "You can read it three times a day, if you like. At least put the original in a safe deposit box. Keeping it at home, Harriet, I don't advise that. It's too risky."

But Harriet was a stubborn woman. "No, Frank," she said, "I appreciate your concern. But I'll keep the original with me, thank you."

"OK, Harriet," I said. "But, for instance: suppose there's a fire?"

"I don't believe in fires," she said. "There'll be no fire."

That was Aunt Harriet. I dropped the subject. I never argue with a client. Especially a client as rich as Harriet Wingate. She took the will with her, in a manila envelope, and it disappeared into a kind of black hole.

2

Aunt Harriet, as I said, lived in a small house—sort of an over-grown cottage—in the city of Palo Alto. It was a two-story house. She lived alone. She could have had a bigger house and a housekeeper, but she wanted privacy and a kind of inde-pendence. Her tastes did not run to the grandiose. Edna, the cleaning lady, came every day (I think), but there was no live-in help. It was a pretty house, neat, well-ordered. I remember the beautiful curtains and drapes—all bright canary yellow; and the yellow wallpaper. It gave the place a cheerful look, all shiny and bright; forward-looking, and even a bit bold. On the other hand, I think some of the furniture was fairly antiquat-ed. Family heirlooms; and perhaps quite valuable. Aunt Har-riet came from a very old family.

"She was a Spively," Karen said to me once. Karen was Barbara's sister. I think I mentioned that.

"Right. A Spively." I didn't know what a Spively was. It could have been anything. It turned out to be the name of a family, the sort of family that knows who its ancestors are.

"Wingate was her married name, of course," Karen said. "She was born a Spively." She could see I was unimpressed. I tried to look as if it meant something to me, but I failed, as I usually do at that sort of thing. Karen went on to tell me, in great detail: "The Spively's came over on the Mayflower. Lit-erally. Peleg Spively was his name, the ancestor. He married Hepzibah Witherspoon. My mother and Aunt Harriet were direct descendants of Peleg and Hepzibah Spively."

For myself, I was the descendant, as far as I know, of a long line of peddlers and nobodies. My ancestors most definitely did *not* come over on the Mayflower. They came on some sort of cattle-boat, I suppose, in the late nineteenth century, one of those boats full of lice and dirt, with zillions of people crammed into the hold of the ship. I suppose they were part of the huddled masses yearning to be free. In any event, I never had much interest in family background. My grandparents died when I was young. That could be one reason. Some people have grandparents who talk a lot about the old days; and maybe that's why they become hooked on genealogy.

Karen, unlike me, was obsessed with the subject. It was one of her chief occupations. "I'm writing a history of the Spively family," she said. "I'm enormously proud of them. It's people like Peleg and Hepzibah who made this country great."

"Did you hear a lot about the Spively's from Aunt Harriet?" I asked.

Karen laughed. "Good grief, no. She couldn't care less. Aunt Harriet had no sense of family history. She despised all that, to tell you the truth. Quite the opposite. She once said to me, Karen, if you dig long enough, you'll find skeletons in the closet. She said, she'd rather not dwell on the past. No, Frank, I'm the only one in the family that really cares. And I do care, deeply. I think family is... almost everything. It's tradition, it's... well, it's in the blood, don't you think?"

I nodded my head in agreement. I always agree with my clients, unless they say something about the law, in which case I set them straight, but gently. I wondered if Karen honestly thought that being a Spively made you better than all those other people, the millions and millions of non-Spively's. I hope not.

But I see I'm digressing. At least you probably *think* I'm digressing. You probably think it doesn't matter to this story that Harriet Wingate was born a Spively. Actually, it does, but that comes a lot later on.

Anyway, I was telling you something about Harriet Wingate's house. I won't bore you with details. The basic facts are these: it was a two-story house, rather conventional. Downstairs was a guest-room, a living room, a kitchen and a half-bath. Upstairs was the main bedroom, which Harriet occupied, also a bathroom, and two small rooms, one of which

Harriet used as a kind of study. Not that she studied anything. But she wrote letters at a desk, and the desk had a locked drawer, in which she kept important papers like her will. Except that the will wasn't there.

I want to mention again the fact that she lived alone. Her husband, Tommy, lived somewhere else. At one time, he did live in the house—in the guest room downstairs. But about a year before Harriet died he moved out. More about this later.

Anyway, Harriet Wingate was all alone when she died. She died in her sleep. Or was murdered, if you believe Barbara's version, in which case she wasn't alone when she died. In the morning, the cleaning lady, Edna, came to the house as usual. She was a heavyset lady—I'd seen her once or twice; a nice woman who had been cleaning for Harriet for years and years. Like so many women who cleaned houses, she had had a miserable life, which she never hesitated to tell you about. Her husband, who drank himself to death. Her oldest son who got in with the wrong crowd, and was sitting in jail. Her daughter's many pregnancies. She lived across the bay and had to travel a long distance to get to Harriet's house. But she liked Harriet; Harriet was good to her.

Anyway, that morning, she let herself in with her key, as usual, and went about her work. But when she got upstairs—well, you can imagine the scene. Harriet Wingate was still lying in bed, completely dead.

It upset Edna and she started screaming and crying, but nobody heard her of course. (Barbara told me this part of the story). Then she calmed down, called a doctor—as if a doctor could do anything with a dead woman—and of course phoned Barbara. Barbara, as it happened, wasn't home; she was with her exercise group at a gym. Then Edna called Karen, told her what had happened; and Karen came right over. Not that there was anything *she* could do. I guess they eventually did contact Barbara—she was home an hour later—and the two of them started calling the other relatives. They also called Tommy, who was, after all, Harriet's husband, and began arranging for the funeral and so on.

Tommy, by the way, played no part in any of the ar-
rangements, the funeral, the family affairs and so on. The two
sisters simply took over. I note that for the record.

I was one of the people they called, and naturally I said
how sorry I was and what a wonderful woman Harriet Wingate had been, and all that; and I expressed my sorrow and my
empathy. I don't want to sound cynical: I really was sorry
Harriet had passed on, and Barbara and Karen felt genuine
grief, I'm sure of that, they were very close, after all; and I
suppose for them it was therapeutic to get down to details, the
funeral, the estate, and the rest of that.

Anyway, Barbara and I went to the house the very next
day—the body had gone to the funeral parlor—I'm not big on
dead bodies; and Barbara and I had breakfast together and
talked about the estate, at least in a general way. The will, at
least the will I drafted, named Barbara as executor. Barbara let
us in with her key—I stress this fact, because it became relevant, later on, to talk about who had a key and who did not.

I was struck by how neat the house was. And how quiet.
Of course it was quiet, but it seemed unnaturally quiet. I know
I'm talking nonsense. If I didn't know that Harriet was dead, it
wouldn't have seemed any different from any other house. But
it gave me a creepy feeling. It seemed so still, so frozen in time,
like a museum. Maybe I'm just being sentimental.

Anyway, that's when we went to look for the will. The Last
Will and Testament of Harriet Wingate. The one I drew up, all
legal and proper. We looked, all over the house. The will was
simply not there. We looked in all the usual places: nothing.
First of all, we went into the study, and looked in the drawers
of the desk. The drawers were locked, but Barbara had a key.
We searched every drawer. We found some papers and letters,
and a deed to the house, but not much of any real interest.

Only one thing: something rather surprising. It had nothing to do with the will. It seems that Harriet Wingate kept,
locked in one of the drawers of her desk, a manila folder, with
newspaper clippings. We were busy searching for a will, but I
couldn't help looking at the clippings, all yellowing with age.
There was, for instance, her late husband's obituary. And a
story, from the local newspaper, about him, two columns long.

And a picture of Joseph Wingate, looking very old. There were other clippings about the family; an item by Karen in a local newspaper, about the Spively family, and how Karen was tracing their ancestry, and so on, all about the fact that there was a southern branch and a New England branch of the Spively's. I barely glanced at this.

But then there was something quite different: old clippings, seven or eight years old, from an Arizona newspaper. One clipping told about a horrendous crime near Phoenix. Two men, a woman, and an adolescent boy had been on a crime spree, robbing stores in and around Phoenix. They were caught but escaped. On the run, they hijacked a car, and kidnapped a young couple with two kids, who had been driving the car. The gang drove out to the desert, and murdered the family or tried to. One of the kids survived to tell the tale. Another clipping told a follow-up story: how the police caught up with the gang, and there was a gun battle, and one of the gang was killed. I couldn't help wondering: how was this connected to Harriet Wingate? Why had she preserved these particular clippings, for so long, in a locked drawer in her desk?

"Did you find anything?" Barbara asked.

I was embarrassed, put down the folder and continued the search. I found nothing; at any rate, no will.

I asked Barbara if anybody else had a key to this dresser and to the drawers. She thought not, but wasn't sure. Anybody besides Harriet Wingate, I mean. Her own key was in a black leather purse, along with her house keys and a lot of the other stuff women carry in their purses. And the purse was right where we expected it to be—in her bedroom.

Not that I thought about foul play or anything of the sort, not at the time. I just wondered why the will wasn't there.

"You don't think somebody stole it?" Barbara asked. "The drawer was locked."

"Right. But that kind of flimsy lock isn't much of an obstacle, not to a professional," I said. Of course I didn't know what I was talking about. For me, the lock would have been an insuperable obstacle.

"Where *could* that will be?" Barbara asked.

Well, one obvious answer would be: in Harriet's safe deposit box. Or boxes: she had two of them, in two different banks in Palo Alto, one on California Avenue, another on El Camino Real. The vault keys were in a little envelope, in that desk drawer. We had no trouble getting entry, because the boxes were in the joint names of Harriet Wingate and Barbara Homans.

"I didn't have the key, actually," Barbara said. "But Aunt Harriet wanted my name on these boxes, in case something happened to her. And... something did," she said, and reached for her handkerchief. She began sobbing quietly.

I find grief very embarrassing. I don't know how to deal with it. It's a male deficiency—I know that. My wife Celia is much better at situations of this kind; she knows how to behave. Anyway, we checked out both boxes. In each bank, we took the box into the little cubicles they give you, and we examined everything inside the box. We made lists and catalogued everything. There were stocks and bonds. Some of the stock certificates were quite old and beautiful. Wonderful engravings. Nowadays, a person's portfolio has been reduced to electronic blips. The poetry is gone. Harriet had arranged everything neatly. There were also all sorts of legal documents: a copy of Joseph Wingate's death certificate, in an envelope, along with a yellowed clipping from the newspaper—another version of his obituary. There were also deeds to various pieces of real estate—all of them sold by now. But in neither bank, in neither safe deposit box, was there the slightest sign of anything like a will.

Of course, Aunt Harriet might have torn the will up. There's always that possibility. She had taken it home, against my advice; and she could have destroyed it. You can do that, you know. Nothing to it, and it's perfectly legal. You just tear the will to pieces, or you burn it, you throw it out in the trash, or you flush it down the toilet. That's the end of the will, legally speaking. You've revoked it, as we lawyers say.

She could have done one of those things. In that case, the will would be gone without a trace. But somehow I doubted this. Aunt Harriet was very careful about financial and legal affairs. I'm sure she would have told me about it—she would have called me on the phone, at the very least, and told me what she had done.

This is the way I felt at the time—the way I felt when Barbara and I left Bank No. 2, and the realization sank in that there was no will to be found *anywhere*; that, as far as we knew, she died without a will. As you'll see, I was wrong about many, many things—things having to do with Harriet Wingate, and about other people too. But at the time, I was simply puzzled and confused.

Suppose she hadn't torn up her will; in that case, what could have happened to the blasted thing? You don't just go around losing wills. They're too precious. Too important. But whatever happened, the brute fact remained: we had no will in front of us.

We had been discussing this very situation, in my office, just before Barbara brought up her strange idea: the idea that somebody killed Aunt Harriet. Aunt Harriet had been dead a few weeks, as I told you. Of course, the will issue had surfaced very quickly. We had to open an estate for Harriet—a will might turn up later. I had my doubts; but this was an estate of millions of dollars, and we had to do *something*. So I did open an estate, and I persuaded the court to appoint Barbara as the administrator, at least on a temporary basis.

She was, after all, a close relative. Tommy, the surviving spouse, under the law, had the right to serve as administrator; but apparently he didn't want to, and he was perfectly happy to let Barbara have the job. That's what Barbara told me, and she had Tommy write me a note, saying he declined to serve. The note was scrawled, in big letters, the way a fifth grader would write. Half the words were misspelled. Tommy, I gathered, was no genius.

Anyway, that was the situation we were facing. The estate had to be opened, and there was a lot of business to be taken care of, will or no will. I explained to Barbara what her duties were, what to do about dividends, how she could pay bills, and out of what account. How to handle the whole estate, in other words. She listened and took notes. When I was more or less done with my spiel, that's when Barbara dropped her bombshell.

"Wait a minute," I said, "do you think the missing will is... well, connected to this, uh, *theory* of yours?"

"This *theory*?"

"This idea. This suspicion. What you just told me," I said.

"I absolutely do. Somebody tore up that will or stole it. And it wasn't Aunt Harriet," she said.

"But who would do a thing like that?" I asked.

"Ah, that's the question," she said. "But *somebody* did. I just *know* she kept the will in that dresser drawer. It just had to be there. And you said yourself, it wouldn't be much of a trick to break into that drawer. Who knows? Anybody who came in the house might have gotten hold of that will."

"But who was that? Who came into the house?"

"Well: Tommy for one," she said.

"Tommy? Her husband?"

"Naturally. He had a key."

But this didn't seem very likely to me. Why would Tommy steal her will and tear it up? The will left him half the estate. He and Aunt Harriet had not been married very long and California is a community property state. He was entitled to half the community property; but I didn't think that would amount to much. Basically, tearing up the will would probably make him much worse off.

"He doesn't have a motive," I said. "That will left him millions of dollars."

"Did he know that?"

"Well, if he stole the will, he could read it, couldn't he? And he'd see it there, in black and white."

"It didn't say, I leave millions of dollars to Tommy."

"It gave him, roughly, half the estate. He could figure out that was real money. He must have known Harriet was rich."

"Well, he could have had a reason."

"Maybe," I said. "Who else had access to the house?"

"Frank, I don't know. I did. Edna did. There could have been other people. Karen, for one."

"Did Karen have a key?"

"Karen wouldn't do a thing like that."

"I didn't say she would."

"Anyway," Barbara said. "I'm not sure she had a key. But it could have been some other visitor. How would I know who came and went at Aunt Harriet's?"

How indeed. The question was: who gained if the will was destroyed? Not Barbara and Karen: like Tommy, they lost a lot of money in the process. So did the friends who would have gotten something under the will. If no will showed up, then Harriet Wingate died intestate, as the legal term goes. Tommy would get a share. I'd have to look up exactly how much, and the rest I suppose would go to all the nieces and nephews, because they were the closest living kin. I'm not sure how many there were. Harriet Wingate had had a sister, Barbara's mother, now dead. There were two brothers, older brothers, and both of *them* were dead. The nieces and nephews were scattered all over—Sydney Australia, Cincinnati, other exotic places. Karen and Barbara were the only ones who lived in the Bay Area. I think I told you that.

I made a mental note to check the California Probate Code and confirm this, I mean that the nieces and nephews would get the estate. I work with the Code all the time; I do a lot of estates work, maybe more of that line of work than anything else, but I certainly don't know the Code by heart. It's a thousand pages long. Most of it, of course, is incredibly dull. Maybe all of it. Nobody reads the Probate Code for pleasure.

"You're awfully quiet," Barbara said. "What are you thinking about?"

"The will... or rather that there isn't any will," I said.

"I know. It's a mystery, isn't it?" she said.

"It's not *like* Harriet. To be so careless with a thing like that. Not like her at all."

"You're right. I mean, it's really all wrong. Aunt Harriet would never, never let that happen. Not to have a will. She wanted us—me and Karen—to have the money. I'm sure of that. I'm totally convinced somebody got in and tore up the will."

She was right about Harriet's wishes. When we discussed her will, she made it crystal clear: she wanted Barbara and her sister Karen to have half the estate. She also definitely wanted to leave money to Tommy. That was equally clear; but I didn't stress this point. Barbara had said nothing about Tommy.

"Barbara," I said, "I know what you're saying. But... it's a serious thing, to tear up somebody's will."

"Very serious, I'm sure. So is stealing and murder and so on, but they happen."

"That's true," I said. "Not that I've ever come across such a thing, I mean, where somebody deliberately tore up somebody else's will. Not in all my years as a lawyer."

"There's a first time for everything," she said.

"It's weird, I admit it," I said. "Still, Aunt Harriet did some weird things, didn't she?"

"Weird things? What sorts of things?"

I was going to mention marrying somebody 60 years her junior, but I held my tongue. This might be a sore subject. "Never mind.... Anyway, there's nothing we can do about the will. And, frankly, we can't do anything about your idea that somebody murdered your aunt."

"You're telling me to forget it? Not to do anything about it?"

"I guess I am. Unless something else comes up, something more specific."

"Honestly, Frank!" she said; her voice dripped disappointment. But what else could I do or say? Murder was hardly my specialty. And this wasn't even murder... at least, I didn't think so. Just an old lady, dying in her sleep. We changed the subject, talked more about the estate, the assets, what Barbara's role was going to be, and so on.

She left around five o'clock. I had to see another client, who had been waiting impatiently for me in the outer office. I spent about half an hour with the client. I did a little bit of paperwork, then I hurried home for dinner.

Celia had invited some guests to join us. Celia teaches in the local high school. The assistant principal, whose name was Jerry something—I forget his last name—came with his wife, Marilyn, who was very fat. Fat, and extremely quiet. Jerry Something always did all of the talking. Celia made a fish stew.

It was one of her specialties. Some people don't like fish; but she felt that was their problem, not hers.

I rushed home, because it would be unfair to Celia if I came too late to help out; even worse if I arrived after the guests did. When I got home, Celia was frantically working. She was behind schedule and I had to pitch in immediately, cutting carrots and cucumbers and tossing the salad. The evening was boring, but distracting. Celia and Jerry Something talked, or rather gossiped, about what went on at the school. Marilyn and I were basically furniture. But for the time being at least, I forgot all about Barbara, Aunt Harriet, and the missing will.

The next day, however, I got a strange phone call from a lawyer named Peter Elver, and the case of Harriet Wingate took the first of many surprising turns.

3

I think I told you I was a lawyer. I am. Don't hold it against me. It's an honorable profession. That's what they tell you in law school. The public apparently thinks otherwise. Public opinion polls are very discouraging. People seem to think *most* lawyers are thieves and parasites. In the Gallup poll, the public ranks lawyers under absolutely everybody, except maybe members of Congress and used car salesmen.

I suppose every profession has its rotten apples. Do we have more than our share?

The funny thing about polls and the legal profession: people don't like or trust lawyers in general, but they do like, and do trust, their *own* lawyer. That's what the research shows. Probably they feel the same way about members of Congress. I'm not sure about used car salesmen.

I'm a lawyer in private practice. I'm what's called a solo. I have no partners. I don't work for one of those huge law factories—some of them have thousands of lawyers, an appalling thought. I don't work for a company either. I'm all alone. I have a small office in San Mateo, California. It's in one of those low-rise stucco buildings, mostly full of dentists. I don't mind dentists. The world needs them. People are not wild about dentists, but they need them. Lawyers are in the same general category.

What else can I tell you? I'm 45 years old. Depending on who you are, that's very old or very young or very in between. I won't bother describing myself. I'm quite ordinary in looks. Anyway, that's what I think I see in the mirror. I do like my eyes. I have dark brown eyes. I have no particular opinion about my nose or my chin. I'm starting to get slightly bald. It bothers me, but only a little.

I'm neither fat nor thin. More or less. To be honest, if you saw me with my clothes off, a privilege you are unlikely to have, you'd notice a definite paunch. But not a serious one; nothing a bulky sweater can't cover up. I tried to figure out my body mass once, but it was too discouraging. I exercise every once in a while. Celia and I bought a treadmill, but I don't use it very much. I mean, "on a treadmill" is a metaphor for a depressing, repetitive rut. Why would anybody choose a depressing, repetitive rut of their own free will?

My treadmill has nothing to do with this story. I'll try to stick to the essentials. I have a wife, Celia. I've mentioned her already—two teenaged daughters, a small but nice house, a yard, rose-bushes, and two cars. I don't have a dog. I've never cared that much for dogs.

My house is in Menlo Park, California, which isn't very far from my office—it's a bit further south, down the peninsula. I live in a nice neighborhood. Middle-class people. None of my neighbors, to the best of my knowledge, is an ax-murderer, or a registered sex offender. There was a murder, come to think of it, down the block; but it doesn't concern this particular story.

My practice is pretty general. I don't like to turn down any business that comes my way. Within limits, of course. I don't do criminal work; I never have. That's a very specialized line of practice, and I stay away from it. My actual clients are a mixed bag. Some of them are guys who own small businesses: one of them runs a car wash, another has two small restaurants, and still another one manufactures plastic novelties. I represent four or five dentists. They're in my building. Dentistry itself does not produce a lot of law work, but what there is, they give to me.

I litigate when I absolutely have to but I'm not exactly a thrilling court-room orator. Few of us are. The impression of the work of lawyers, the ideas people get from television—well, it's laughably inaccurate. Anyway, a great deal of my work is estate planning and related matters: wills, trusts, guardianships, that sort of thing. I like estates work. It's clean, honest work. It pays the rent, my other expenses, with enough left over for a vacation, contributions to a pension plan, and money to buy clothes for my daughters. Celia works, as I said, so we're a two-income family. In this part of the country, you need that. Peter Elver—the person who called me on the phone—is also a lawyer. He's about my age, mid-40's, maybe a little older. He has an office in Redwood City, California. That's a town a bit north of Menlo Park. It's a little grungier than my town, as a matter of fact. Anyway, Peter has his practice there. Redwood City happens to be the county seat of San Mateo County, in case you're interested.

Peter's not a friend of mine; he's an acquaintance. We've had professional dealings from time to time. Nothing major. He's skinny, and somewhat short—shorter than I am, and I'm average height. He wears a small beard, black tinged with gray and he has a decided facial tic. At times, it seems to get worse. Maybe when he's nervous.

As I said, I didn't know that much about Peter Elver. He seemed to be a perfectly competent lawyer, but who knows. Like me, he does a lot of estates work. He has a big ad in the Yellow Pages announcing his specialty. That's something I would never do. But I don't hold it against him.

I wasn't expecting a call from him, and as far as I know we had no business in common, but still his call was no great surprise. Lawyers call other lawyers all the time. When I heard his voice at the other end of the phone, I simply wondered which one of my clients did *his* client want to sue, and on what issue.

"Frank, it's Peter," he said, "Peter Elver."

"Hi Peter. What's new?"

"Oh, same old business. You know. Getting along."

"Me too."

He made some small talk about mutual acquaintances, and he asked me if I had heard about so-and-so, who had a heart attack. I hadn't heard. Peter seemed to assume that so-and-so, the lawyer with the heart attack, was a bosom buddy of mine. I had no idea where he got that notion.

Then he got to the point: "Frank, I wanted to talk to you about... a client."

"Shoot. What client?"

He cleared his throat. "I'm referring to Harriet Wingate."

"Harriet Wingate? What about her? I'm handling her estate; I suppose you know that. Do you have a claim against her estate?"

"No," he said, "it's something else. Can I come see you tomorrow? I'd like to talk to you in person."

I thought this was odd, a little on the dramatic/mysterious side. He seemed to be suggesting that Harriet had been *his* client, which I thought was impossible. Anyway, I said, "Sure thing." I wondered what this was all about. I could not have guessed the truth in a million years.

4

Peter wanted to see me as soon as possible. Frankly, I often have blocks of free time, but as it happened, the next day was pretty much booked up. We settled on 3:30. I was done talking to a client at about 3:25, and was showing him out when Peter came in. Peter was usually prompt, in my experience. He seemed somewhat nervous, though. The facial tic was very much in evidence. He looked... haggard, older. But then, after all, I didn't see him that often. Maybe *I* looked haggard and older to *him*.

"What's the mystery, Peter?" I asked.

"Mystery?"

"You sounded on the phone like it was some sort of big deal."

I hadn't noticed before how short he was. I would say five foot five. I noticed too that his beard was streaked with more gray than I remembered. He had on a brown suit with the usual conservative tie, and he carried a rather battered brief-case. He held on to it somewhat nervously.

Peter Elver had gone to law school relatively late in life, maybe in his 30's. I don't know what he did before that. Somebody once said he was a court reporter, but I'm not sure. I never thought of him as, well, flourishing. If you're making a lot of money, you're supposed to *look* rich. Peter never looked rich, definitely not. But I suppose he made a living, just as I did. Like me, he did a lot of work with trusts and estates, as I said. Old ladies seemed to like him. At least, I had heard that. He was not the kind who appealed to hot-shots and yuppies, or to venture capitalists and people in the fast lane. They liked more flash and dash. Peter lacked these qualities.

That's not a criticism. Probably I lack these qualities myself.

"You're right. It is a mystery. I came to talk about... Harriet Wingate's will."

"Her will? What will?"

He seemed embarrassed. "Harriet Wingate came to see me," he said. "Some time before she died. She said she wanted to make out a will."

I was dumbfounded. "Harriet Wingate? She came to see *you*?"

"Yes. What's wrong with that?"

"Nothing. It's a free country. It's just... I mean, to be honest, she *was* my client. I had been helping her with her will for... oh, twenty years. Tell me, what was the date?" I asked. "I mean, Peter, when was this? Can you be precise?"

"I can. I checked my records. It was August 2nd."

August 2nd! And Harriet had come to me some time in July to talk about her will. And August 2nd—that was shortly before she died.

I said: "You knew she was my client, didn't you?" I couldn't resist this.

He made a face as if he was chewing on a lemon. "Yes, Frank, I knew that. Well, you know as well as I do, people have the right to change lawyers; and they do from time to time. She... I didn't know her, of course. Never met her. She said she was referred to me by her friend, Gloria Graffin."

The name was vaguely familiar. "Who's that?"

"A client of mine. A woman about Harriet's age. I did some work for her. She and Harriet Wingate were friends. Neighbors too, I think. At any rate, that's what Mrs. Wingate said."

"Go on."

"Harriet Wingate called me, she said she wanted to consult me. Well, why shouldn't I see her? What did I know? Maybe she had a fight with you. Maybe she wasn't satisfied with your work. It happens. I win some clients, I lose some clients. You do too, I'm sure."

"Come off it," I said. "Harriet Wingate and I were on the best of terms."

"I believe you, Frank, but how was I supposed to know that? Anyway, if that was the case, why *did* she come to me? She said she needed a will. And she was in a hurry."

"Did she produce the old will?"

"No. She said she had no will. She said she had one once, but she destroyed it."

This was getting weirder and weirder. "And what kind of will did she want?"

"Pretty simple. She left everything to charity."

"Charity? Nothing to her husband? Nothing to her nieces?"

"Husband? She didn't say anything about a husband. Was she married? I'm sure I asked her about family. It's on my checklist, things I ask my clients.... No, she left nothing to anybody, almost everything to charity."

"What kind of charity?"

"Cats. Abandoned cats. She named some organization, I never heard of it, an organization that does that sort of thing. Takes care of stray cats. I checked it out. It seemed legitimate. That's what she wanted; she was very sure of herself."

I couldn't believe this. "Cats? Did she have cats? I went to her place a couple of times, I never saw a cat. She never even mentioned cats. She had a husband, Peter—you didn't know that? And nieces that she was close to. Two of them in particular, they live in this area. Her will, which she made out in July, that's less than a month before she saw you... that will left half her estate to her husband, and the other half to those nieces."

"Well, I know about the nieces. But she didn't leave them anything. There's no law that says you have to leave money to nieces. Maybe they did something that pissed her off. Who knows? It wasn't any of my business."

He was right of course. "So... she left everything to these cats.... And, well, who did she name as executor?"

He gulped. "Actually, Frank, it was me. I tried to talk her out of it. I said, I don't know you, Mrs. Wingate, we've just met. But she insisted."

I was reeling with these surprises. "You?! Executor? I can't understand it."

"Well, don't go overboard, Frank. It's not like I'm not qualified. I'm a member of the bar; it's not a ridiculous idea. She really insisted. Executor. Oh, and trustee."

"Trustee? Of what?"

He said: "A trust for three cats. She said she had three pet cats, Teddy, Beulah, and Katie. I was supposed to take care of these cats, until they died, and that's when the estate was going to charity."

"And where is this will?"

"I have a copy. She had the original. I said I wanted to keep it, but she wasn't having that. She said she'd keep it with her, at home. I said, that's not a good idea. I said, what if there's a fire?"

I said, "Wait: don't tell me. She said she didn't believe in fires."

"How did you know that, Frank?"

"She used the same line with me."

He looked extremely uncomfortable. I said: "How come you're just telling me this now?"

"I've been away, off and on. I went to visit family, in the East. A week or so, I was gone. I guess I left the day after she died, so... I didn't even know she was dead. When I came back, I had some catching up to do, and somehow the news didn't get to me for a while. Then somebody said Harriet Wingate was dead."

"Who said it? Who would have told you that?"

"A client. I'd rather not say."

I thought that was stupid, not to tell me, but I let it go. Peter went on: "My... client said you were handling the estate. I thought, well that's odd. I should be in on this, I'm the executor, after all. And I have a duty, to find the will, and file it. So... that's why I called you. Where is the will? I don't mean to make a fuss, but I should be the one who handles her affairs. She named me executor."

"The will? The will you're talking about? I have no idea," I said. "I had no notion there *was* such a will. We were looking for a different will. The will she came to me about. We didn't find it. We looked everywhere, the house, her safe deposit box, everywhere. We found nothing, actually. I mean, no will at all."

Peter seemed distressed. "But where is it, then? She executed it, well, it wasn't long before she died. What happened to the document?"

"How should I know, Peter? I suppose she tore it up. It was a crazy idea to begin with."

"Tore it up? I don't think so," he said. "She seemed so certain, so determined. I asked her again and again, is this what you want? She was absolutely sure. Oh yes, she said, this is what I want, I'm an old woman, and I have no close family—those were her very words."

"No close family? Well, Peter, she had these two nieces—they were like daughters to her. Not to mention her husband."

"I told you, she never said boo about a husband."

"Why would she cut him out of the will?"

"Hey, beats me. Maybe they had a pre-nuptial agreement."

"And the nieces?"

"Well, she said she didn't want them to get her money."

"And you accepted that? At face value?"

"What do you mean, Frank? Why shouldn't I accept that? Am I supposed to assume my clients are lying?"

"But as you know, Peter, husbands have rights, will or no will."

"Of course I know that, Frank. I keep telling you, she never said a word about a husband. I did talk to her about... disinheriting her family. You know, she was old, and... there could be a lawsuit, undue influence, or people saying she was senile, but she was very firm: she said there would be no lawsuits, it was impossible."

I said: "That's what they all say, there's no problem. It's your job to see to it that they're right."

"Frank, you don't have to preach to me. I went to law school, too, you know. But in the end, it has to be what the client wants, doesn't it?"

"Alright, alright," I said. "Let's not wrangle. Anyway, it doesn't matter. The will is gone."

"That's what I don't understand."

"Well, Peter," I said, a little testily, "what part of it don't you understand? Gone means gone."

"But what happened to it? To change your mind, so soon? To go to all that trouble, and then tear it up, or something...."

"People do crazy things," I said, "you should know that by now. You've got clients, you know what I mean. They do totally crazy things. Nothing surprises me anymore."

This wasn't quite accurate. Some things do surprise me. And Harriet Wingate's visit to Peter Elver was more than a surprise. It was a bombshell.

5

My mind was racing around and around like a rabbit chased by a fox. I wouldn't say this out loud to Peter, but I was completely mystified. Mystified by the late Harriet Wingate, and her really peculiar behavior. I couldn't understand why Harriet would desert me for Peter Elver, of all people; and why she would leave everything she owned to a bunch of cats. Nobody had ever mentioned cats before. Nobody. There were no cats in the picture, until now.

Still, if Peter was telling the truth—and nobody could invent such a stupid story—then there *had* been another will, a peculiar will to be sure; but a will after all is a will. And there were, in fact, people with a very strong motive for getting rid of that will. For that matter, they had a very strong motive for getting rid of Aunt Harriet, if it came to that.

Take Barbara and her sister, Karen. The cat will cost them the entire estate. They would end up with absolutely nothing. Everything would go to the cats.

Tommy? Well, he was Harriet's lawful husband, I suppose, and he would still get something, even if the will cut him out. But did he know that? If he saw a will lying around the house, a will that left him nothing, and left everything to some stupid cats, would he really understand his rights under California law? Most people wouldn't.

Suppose Harriet Wingate had torn up the old will, the will that I drew up, and then made out this new one. Suppose one of those three found out. Harriet took the will home, after all; she put it in her drawer. The drawer was locked, but still....

What if Barbara or Karen or Tommy saw the will? They'd see millions of dollars flying out the window.

Still, I found it hard to buy this theory. I couldn't imagine Barbara tearing up a will, let alone killing somebody. She was my *client*. She seemed so middle class, so ordinary. I didn't know Karen very well. But she was Barbara's sister, and the little I knew of her, she didn't strike me as the kind that would tear up a will. Or murder her aunt. Spively's, I suppose, are not supposed to kill people.

That left Tommy. I'd never really met Tommy. I'd seen him at the funeral, but we never exchanged any words. But here was a 23 year old guy, married to a woman old enough to be his grandmother, or even older; maybe that kind of guy was capable of anything. *If* somebody killed the old woman—and that was still a mighty big if—I suppose Tommy had to be the prime candidate. And he had to be the prime candidate, if somebody found and tore up the will. *If* there was such a person, another big if.

Still, the whole thing was just so bizarre. Harriet Wingate had a perfectly good will, a perfectly ordinary will. She left money to her husband, which seems normal, even if you don't have a normal husband; bits and chunks to friends and relatives, also quite normal; and the rest to her two favorite nieces, women who were like daughters to her. Then, suddenly, she changes her mind, drops her lawyer, goes to a strange lawyer, and tells him she wants to leave everything to cats. Why? I can imagine getting mad at one person, and cutting them out of a will: but all three? And this sudden conversion to cats—this passion for cats? Out of the blue. It didn't make sense.

Some people, I know, are absolutely crazy about cats. They have whole houses full of cats, meowing and purring and scratching the furniture. Or dogs. People are insane about dogs. Or box turtles, for that matter. Or tropical fish. I have a client who has five parakeets at home. I also have clients who come to the office with their big slobbering dogs, the dogs are like members of the family. They treat them better than they treat human beings. And I had this woman client, a professional woman: she had this green-eyed cat she adored, she brought it with her every time she entered my office; she stroked the thing incessantly and called it Poopsie.

But Harriet Wingate? She didn't seem the type.

Teddy, Beulah, and Katie. Three cats with a trust fund. Ridiculous. I kept trying to remember the times I had been in Harriet's house. I never saw any cats in the house. I never saw any *signs* of a cat—no cat food, no scratches on the furniture or those disgusting boxes filled with kitty litter. Was it possible she had suddenly developed this mania for cats? Out of the blue? I remembered, I had been in the house after Harriet died, helping Barbara hunt for the will. No cats. No trace of cats at all. What could this cat business mean?

I realized that while I had been lost in thought, Peter was still talking. I hadn't heard a word. "I'm sorry, Peter, would you repeat that?" He was still talking about the will. Now he was going on and on about the procedures for probating lost wills, about trying to get the court to recognize the cat will, of which, of course, he had a copy. "You aren't seriously considering that, are you?" I asked.

"I guess I am."

"It's nonsense," I said.

"Oh, it's very far from nonsense," he said. "There's a lot of money involved."

"I warn you, we'll fight it," I said. "And it won't work. Do you know how hard it is to make out a case like that? Have you ever actually tried it?"

"No, but...."

"Well, just read the Probate Code: the presumption is, if you can't find the will, that she got rid of the will herself. People do that all the time. Tear up a will, I mean."

"I *have* looked at the Probate Code, thank you very much. I know what it says as well as you do. And I've been in touch with this cat society," he said. "Frank, as you know, the estate is big: millions. It's worth a shot for them; maybe we can settle."

A big estate also means big fees—I knew this, Peter knew this, and it made the conversation a little bit edgy. If he could establish the validity of this ridiculous will about cats, he would also presumably handle the estate. He would act as executor and call the shots. Of course, he was not entitled to collect double fees—he had to choose between the executor's slice, and a lawyer's slice. But either one would be a nice pot of gravy. And I could see my own fees flying out the window.

Was he bluffing, or was he serious? Hard to tell.

I sat there, thinking irrelevant thoughts. The Wingate estate was the biggest one that had come my way in a number of years. There are quite a few billionaires in Silicon Valley. But they're all 30 years old and brilliantly healthy. They work out in their private gyms. I'll die before they do. And besides, they have their own crew of lawyers, big-time lawyers.

I had been—OK, I admit it—salivating at the thought of the fees from Harriet's estate. I'm being honest. A lawyer can't help thinking mercenary thoughts. Don't get me wrong. I liked Harriet. And I'm sorry she's dead. Also, I'm a very ethical lawyer. There are such people, believe it or not. But I am definitely not indifferent to money. Who is? Maybe Mother Teresa was. But very few members of the bar.

Mother Teresa never practiced law in California. She took care of lepers. In that department, there's not much cut-throat competition. Peter sat there for a while saying nothing. I had nothing to say either. I tapped on the desk with a pencil. He was right about one thing. There *is* a procedure for probating a will that is lost, or has been destroyed in a fire, for example. Was he seriously thinking of trying that? There was not a shred of evidence that this cat will qualified as a lost or stolen will. It was simply gone. Getting it accepted was, at best, a long shot.

It just wouldn't work. But if it did... I thought: I had better call Celia and tell her not to count on the fee from the Wingate estate. I should tell her to put on hold her plans for redoing the front bathroom. Celia wanted to put in a skylight; I personally saw no need for this skylight. I lived for years and years—basically all of my married life—in that house, and I spent a great deal of time in that bathroom, and I never missed a skylight. But Celia really wanted to do it: "It's so cheerful, and it lets in so much light," she said. I felt the bathroom was already very cheerful. Bathrooms usually are. Bright colors and all that. But I didn't resist very hard.

She also wanted new tile for the bathroom floor. She said: "The old tile is full of scratches." I said, "it isn't." Then she showed me the scratches. I said, "OK, if you lie on the floor of the bathroom, with your nose down, you can see the scratches. But otherwise you can't."

I was winning this battle, I think, until Harriet Wingate died and I mentioned how much money it might be worth to process the estate. That ended the matter. I said to Celia we could call it the Harriet Wingate Memorial Bathroom, and put in a plaque to that effect.

And now... was Peter Elver going to get that money? Along with the home for stray cats? Probably not. But the situation had become definitely more iffy.

Peter said: "A penny for your thoughts."

"Peter, I don't have any thoughts. At any price. I can't believe you want to do this."

"It's my duty," he said.

"Your *duty*? What kind of crap is that?"

"Duty to a client. Yes."

I gave him a look to show what I thought of this outburst of ersatz professional ethics. Was he bluffing? He had come to me, no doubt, all excited. He too had visions of sugarplums dancing in his head. Did his wife want a skylight, too?

He must have been disappointed to learn that the will had disappeared. But surely Peter, an experienced estate lawyer, would have gone to the family first to find out whether the will had turned up, and where it was, since Harriet had taken it with her. Instead he came to me. Why? He said he heard I was handling the estate. Who did he hear it from?

And now *his* will was gone. The cat will. Was he seriously going to try to bring the will back to life? An uphill battle at best.

Of course, nothing was resolved at this meeting. This was just a preliminary visit: it was like two dogs, sniffing each other before they got down to serious fighting. We ended cordially enough. He asked me about my family, how they were. I said, fine. I was going to ask him about *his* family, but I realized I knew nothing about it; I vaguely recalled a rumor that his wife had dumped him some time before. Maybe she took up with somebody whose house already had a skylight. We shook hands and he said goodbye.

6

When Peter left, I realized I had to let Barbara know what had happened. I thought the phone was not the appropriate medium. Anyway, when I called her, nobody seemed to be home, and I left her a message: "Barbara, there's been some new developments.... I mean, about your aunt's estate. Could you come see me tomorrow? Call me, at your earliest convenience."

When I got to the office the next day, there was a message from Barbara on *my* voicemail: "Frank," it said, "you sounded very mysterious. Of course I'll come. Is two o'clock OK? If not, leave a message." Two o'clock, as it happens, was just fine.

There's a lot to be said for voicemail and answering machines. They have their faults, I know. But the virtues far outweigh these vices. Take the problem of calling my mother, who is 84, hard of hearing, and lives in Los Angeles. She accuses me of never calling. She says, "Frank, you never call." Of course, I *do* call from time to time. To tell the truth, half the time she doesn't hear the phone. But if she isn't home, or is in the bathroom, or just doesn't hear me, then I leave her a message and it makes me feel I've done my duty. Of course *she* doesn't think I've done my duty, but then again, she never does.

Barbara came promptly at two. I was done with my last client, and I brought her right in and sat her down.

"Well, Frank?"

I got straight to the point: "Barbara, I had a visit from a lawyer. His name is Peter Elver. He came to see me about your aunt's estate. Believe it or not, there was another will. I said 'was.' We never saw it, and it's disappeared along with the first will."

"Another will? What did you say his name was, this lawyer? I didn't quite catch it."

"Peter Elver."

Barbara screwed up her face. "I never heard of him. Aunt Harriet went to him?"

"That's what he says."

"I don't believe it. She would have told me...."

"But she did go to him, Barbara, and she didn't tell you, I'm sorry to say. And she didn't tell me, either. I was absolutely dumbfounded, when this guy walked in the door with this story. According to him—and it's hard to imagine he made up such a complicated lie—she went to see him, gave him instructions, and made out a brand-new will. That was, oh, not that long before she died. And it was a mighty strange will, believe me!"

"Strange? What was strange about it, Frank?"

"Well, she cut you out, for one thing. And your sister, too. And Tommy, for that matter."

"You can't be serious."

"I'm just telling you what this lawyer said. According to him, your aunt left everything to some society that takes care of abandoned cats. Oh yes, she left a trust fund to take care of three favorite cats, Teddy, Beulah, and Katie. Her pets."

"Is this some kind of joke?"

"If it is, I'm not the one who's telling it. This Peter... OK, he's not the world's greatest lawyer, or the most successful, but he does have a practice, and he specializes in this kind of work. He's got an office in Redwood City. I can't imagine he would make this up. Anyway, he kept a copy of the will."

Barbara looked me straight in the eye. "Frank, Aunt Harriet never had a cat. She hated cats. She was allergic to cats. She couldn't even stay in the same room with a cat. Cats made her sick, literally sick.... She would break out in hives. As long as I knew her, she was that way. She *couldn't* have made out such a will. She absolutely couldn't."

I didn't know what to say. I certainly thought the cat idea was strange, and I had never seen the slightest sign of a cat.

But Barbara's statement was so emphatic. "She didn't even have a goldfish," Barbara said. "My aunt had no pets at all."

"Teddy, Beulah, and Katie? Her three pet cats?"

"They don't exist. I practically *lived* with Aunt Harriet. I called her every day, I was there three or four times a week. I was at the house the day after she died.... And remember, you came with me, to the house, after the funeral, when we hunted for the will. Did you see any cats? Of course you didn't. There were no cats. There *never* were any cats."

She was right, of course. She had to be right. It's easy to tell when a house has pets in it. Dogs especially, but cats are also pretty obvious.

It was getting weirder and weirder. For me, and for Barbara. "Frank," she said. "I don't get it. Something's crazy here."

"I think so too."

"Why would she do this? Is it some kind of code?" Barbara asked. "Was she trying to send a message?"

"A message? Who to? Nobody knew about this will, except this guy Peter."

"I just can't understand it, Frank... This is so upsetting. You think you know somebody intimately. Aunt Harriet was like a mother to me. And then she does something like this. This will, the one with the cats, it cuts me out, altogether? And Karen too? Is that what you're saying?"

"Yes, but don't worry about it. We never found this will, any more than we found the will *I* made out. It's gone— vanished, disappeared."

"Gone?"

"Well, we weren't looking for it, but we certainly never saw it. It wasn't in the house. You were with me. It wasn't in that drawer. Or in her safe deposit boxes. We looked at all her papers. So where is it? Same place the other will is, I suppose: lost in space."

She looked at me helplessly. She opened her purse and took out a handkerchief. Oh God, I thought, she's going to cry. She did. I waited patiently for her to stop. She said, "I'm sorry, Frank. It's just... oh, I can't explain it."

"Barbara," I asked, a bit lamely, "was Aunt Harriet getting, well, a little funny toward the end? I mean, you know, she was in her 80's, and at that age, well, some people start getting less sharp."

"Funny? Aunt Harriet? Less sharp?"

"You know. Not... right. Old people...."

"You mean senile?" I could hear the bite in her voice. "Aunt Harriet? Absolutely not. I saw her the day she died. She was as sharp as ever, as full of life. No, Frank. I absolutely reject any such idea. No. There's something peculiar here, something weird, and I don't know what it is."

I wish I had something concrete to offer, but I was completely out of ideas. I tried to make Barbara feel better about the situation, but it wasn't easy. The lost wills had clearly upset her. I can't blame her for that. It wasn't just the money, although that had to be a factor. It was Harriet's mysterious behavior.

7

When Barbara left my office, I sat at my desk, playing with a pencil, and turning things over and over in my mind. I came up with nothing. Well, almost nothing. I hadn't wanted to repeat this to Barbara, but I kept coming back to Harriet Wingate's mental state. True, whenever I saw her, she seemed fine, alert, on top of things. And Barbara was so insistent on this point. She simply refused to hear any aspersions on Aunt Harriet's mental state.

Still, you read so much about Alzheimer's these days. If you live to be 90, somebody told me, you have a 50-50 chance of getting it. Your brain turns to aluminum foil, or something like that. I think it's something people absolutely dread. I hope somebody puts me out of my misery before I start drooling and staring into space. I stare into space right now, but the drooling is still far in the future. At least I hope so.

Maybe Harriet was in the early stages of Alzheimer's. Maybe she was losing it, but still coping well enough so that she could fool her niece. She *was* an eccentric woman, after all. Take this matter of her and Tommy. I mean, is it ageism to think that when a woman marries a man 60 years younger, something is a little bit off?

Maybe. Maybe not. I suppose what's even stranger is for a young guy to marry a woman in her 80's. Maybe Tommy was the one with the loose screw. Who knows.

Then again, Harriet Wingate was a very rich woman, a woman with pots and pots of money. Maybe that's what Tommy was after: maybe he wasn't such a fool after all.

I've heard of somewhat similar cases. Old women who fall victims to younger men. They become infatuated. Old men too, can fall victim to young women, predator women. I seem to remember that Groucho Marx was one of those victims. Georgia O'Keeffe, the artist: there's another example. I read an article about this once. People get very old and they fall into the clutches of a younger predator. Of any sex.

One of my clients went to court to get herself appointed a kind of guardian for her mother, who was 91. The old woman had money, but she had gotten very confused. She was giving away everything but the kitchen sink, to her neighbors, to two men who came to fix the bathroom toilet, and even to strangers on the street. She took money out of the bank and handed it out on the streets. A woman who worked at the bank called my client. At the rate the old lady was going, nothing would be left by the time she died. Was Harriet Wingate on the road to dementia?

Who knows.

I had no answer to this question. I spent some time thinking and staring into space (without the drooling), but the hurly-burly of everyday life soon interrupted me. I got entangled in the usual web, which in my case means clients. I like my work, although sometimes clients can drive you crazy. Sometimes I dream about winning the lottery and getting rid of the whole lot of them. Still, right now I need them to maintain my stand-ard of living, pay down the mortgage, and keep my family happy.

So I plunged into the intensely boring affairs of the cur-rent crop of clients: first, a young woman climbing the slippery pole in Silicon Valley who wanted to make the climb without her current husband; second, a middle-aged Armenian immi-grant, a self-made man with "properties," as he put it, who wanted to disinherit his worthless son, a young man he de-scribed as grunge. I listened to his screed, as he fulminated about "young peoples," and how they had no respect, no morals, and so on. I thought he would never leave. Next came the tax problems of an old client who owned two restaurants, and whose books and accounts, for tax purposes, were—well, let's call them primitive.

It was only when I got home that I could relax, read the newspaper, watch TV, and in vacant moments, reconsider the problem of Harriet Wingate's estate.

We had supper in the kitchen, Celia and I. The two girls, my teenaged daughters, were off as usual with friends. The house was quiet; I liked that. The girls are OK, I guess, but they spend a lot of time listening to something they call "music," but which sounds to me like loud, vulgar, stupid noise. At least they get good grades, and neither one, as far as I can tell, seems pregnant or likely to get pregnant. What more can a father ask these days?

Deep down they love us, I think; but at this point in their lives, Celia and I are totally utterly awesomely irrelevant, to use their own adverbs. We are a different species. In their eyes, we're androids—people from another planet. Or maybe we're furniture: inanimate but necessary objects that sit still, or should sit still, in the background. Something to park yourself on, eat at, or store things in.

I sat in the kitchen, staring at my plate, and toyed with yesterday's beef stew, prepared straight from the microwave. Celia teaches school, and she works hard. Nobody expects her to come home and magically put something on the table that would make a Julia Child smack her lips.

"Frank, you're not talking to me," she said.

"Sorry." She was right. I wasn't talking to her. Or listening, for that matter. She was telling me something about the principal of her school, about forms to fill out, and about some wretched student in her class who was making her life miserable. I nodded my head. From time to time, I made a comment. Exactly what I said, I have no idea.

The secret of a long marriage is to keep talking. That's essential. I mean *literally* talking. You don't actually have to *say* anything. You certainly don't have to express genuine feelings and thoughts. I mean, *I* don't have to, because I'm a male. Men simply can't do those things. That's been proven by scientific research. They just can't. Only women can. But still, you have to say *something*. You have to seem involved. If your wife wants to redo the bathroom, and she asks you whether you like blue tile or green tile, you have to give an answer. "I don't care" won't do. "Whatever you want, honey," is almost as bad as "I don't care." You have to say "blue." And emphatically, as if you meant it; as if you've thought the matter over very, very carefully. Of course, she'll pick green, but it doesn't matter. You were *involved*.

We have a good marriage: we're comfortable with each other. It's like a right shoe and a left shoe. That's the way we are. We fit each other. I wouldn't have it any other way.

I'm wandering off the subject. That's a mistake. When I read about Kelsey Milhone and the characters in other mystery novels, I skip the parts about her love life and how she put on a spandex thing and went jogging and what she ate for breakfast. I'm only interested in the case, the murder, the mystery.

Back to Harriet Wingate. I couldn't get her out of my mind. I tried to do my mental homework, to sit and just think about it. You know, the little gray cells. But nothing happened in the little gray cells. They failed me completely.

By now I was exhausted. I dragged myself off to bed, after we watched the late local news. Why we watch it I have no idea. Neither of us really cares about the six-car accident in Gilroy or the fire in Vallejo or the updates on the fire or the accident or the flooded basements in the delta.

I lay in bed, but I just couldn't sleep. It kept going around and around in my mind.

Cats. I couldn't believe it. Cats.

And Tommy... Tommy. He was, I realized, really important. I had to talk to Tommy. Somebody pointed him out to me at Harriet's funeral. He came to his wife's funeral—can you imagine?—arm in arm with his current girlfriend. Well, that's California for you. At least that's what my mother would say. She associates California with everything that's completely insane.

Tommy: he was wearing a gray suit, and a necktie, and he looked very uncomfortable, as if this kind of clothing was completely foreign, like a Halloween costume. I remember that he had dark blonde hair which he wore in a ponytail, and a more or less vacant look on his face. He wore dark glasses. It wouldn't surprise me if he was tattooed somewhere or had body piercings in various awkward places. He looked like the type.

On the other hand, there was nothing wrong with his attitude, as far as I could see. He looked pretty solemn, even sad. He came up to the coffin, and put a flower on it, a rose, I think. Was he really feeling grief over Harriet Wingate? As far as I know they were legally married. But whether this was just a charade, I didn't know. I couldn't imagine a roaring sex life, to put it crudely.

The girlfriend: that was another story. She looked pretty good, at least at a distance. She had dark hair, and she seemed a bit older than Tommy. She wore her full, glossy hair quite long, I remember that much. I didn't catch her name. I think Barbara said they were living together. Was Tommy the key to this whole thing? If this cat will was valid, he stood to lose a lot of money. He certainly had every reason to want to tear up that will. And I suppose he had the opportunity. No doubt he was entitled to go in and out of Harriet's house as he pleased: they were husband and wife (or whatever) after all. I suppose he had a key.

Unless the cat will turns up or Peter brings a lawsuit, I'm in charge of the estate. Barbara had been appointed administrator, and I'm her lawyer. No reason why I shouldn't call Tommy, talk to him, get to know him. Tommy *is* the next of kin, the surviving spouse.

The thought was comforting somehow.... It made me think I was *doing* something, moving, heading toward a goal. I'll get in touch with Tommy, get his angle. It's my duty, after all. With this thought in mind, I managed to drift off to sleep.

8

The next day was bright and sunny, but that's nothing unusual or surprising. In California, at least. I got to the office a bit later than usual, plunged into some paperwork, read my email, and treated myself to a cup of coffee. I worked for a while on a draft of a will. Then I took a welcome break, had another coffee, and started thinking about my strategy: how to approach Tommy Wingate. What was I going to say to him?

But to my surprise, Tommy called *me* that very morning.

"Mr. May, this is Tommy Wingate," he said.

"Oh yes, Mr. Wingate. I've been meaning to call you myself. About your, uh, wife's estate."

"Yeah. I know. I heard you were taking care of stuff. The estate I mean. I heard it from Karen. She told me about it. There's something I got to talk to you about. It could be important."

"Right, Mr. Wingate. We do have to talk."

He said, "Call me Tommy. Everybody calls me Tommy."

"OK, Tommy. The reason I was going to call...."

He interrupted. "I've got something here, I've got to show it to you. Harriet gave it to me. It's sealed. It's in a sealed thing, an envelope. She said, 'Tommy, don't open this up, promise?' I promised her. So... well, I didn't open it."

"An envelope? What's inside of it?"

"Mr. May, I don't know. I told you, I didn't open it. Like I said, she made me promise."

"Tommy, you can call me Frank. It's OK."

"Uh... OK."

But in fact he didn't call me Frank. Not right away, any-way. He dropped the "Mr. May," but he didn't replace it with "Frank." He didn't call me anything. I didn't make an issue out of this.

He said he wanted to come see me, because he wanted to give me this document. "Harriet, she said to me, Tommy, if anything happens to me, I want you to give it to the lawyer. I said, what lawyer? She said, the lawyer that's going to handle my estate. I said, what's his name? I think she told me, but maybe she didn't."

"She didn't tell you my name?"

"Maybe she did. I don't remember. Maybe she just said the lawyer. It was a while ago."

I wasn't quite sure what to make of this. Harriet Wingate knew me for at least ten years. She certainly knew my name. Wouldn't she say "Frank May" to this guy? Maybe she did, and it just went in one ear and out the other.

Or did she deliberately leave things ambiguous? Maybe she had torn up the will I drafted for her, so that Barbara was no longer executor, and I was no longer in the picture. In that case, maybe she had somebody else in mind. Could she have meant Peter Elver? But Tommy obviously knew nothing about Peter Elver, and neither did Barbara.

Could I be even sure of *that*? Harriet, after all, could have said Peter Elver and this dimwit just forgot. That was certainly possible.

The more I thought about the situation, the more I leaned toward a theory I had rejected: the theory that Harriet Win-gate was simply losing it. It happens, after all. It's all too common. I have an aunt a little younger than Harriet was, a widow, and for the last few years she hasn't known Monday from Tuesday or a horse from a vegetable. It's pathetic. My cousins took care of her for a while, then it just got too hard. They put her in some sort of institution.

"How come you're just getting around to this, Tommy?" I asked. I tried to make this sound innocuous, I didn't want him to think I was criticizing him.

"I... forgot," he said. This was a lie if I ever heard one. But I dropped the subject. I said: "Well, can you come at 4:15? I'm busy until then. Unless you're busy yourself...."

"Hey, me busy?" He laughed. "No way. I'm basically un- employed. I had a job, but that didn't work out. No problem, I'll come see you at 4:15. Just give me an address. Can I park there? I mean, is there a parking lot? Man, I don't need anoth- er ticket; I've got lots of them already."

I gave Tommy the instructions, went back to work, and even got something done. Tommy appeared at about 4:25, that is, only moderately late. That was fine, because the last client I was talking to ran overtime. Her name was Natasha, she was a hotshot woman executive with a firm in Silicon Valley, one of those little companies that makes some sort of software. In some cases, admittedly not that often, the engineers that start these companies turn into total zillionaires. I think I men- tioned her already. Natasha wanted a divorce. She was tired of her husband, and she was having an affair with somebody else.

Frankly, I don't know when she had time for sex with *anybody*. She seemed to work twenty hours a day; her life was absolutely frantic. Maybe she had sex instead of lunch. She was certainly thin enough to make this a logical guess.

Anyway, she wanted a divorce. Her husband was not as cooperative as she had hoped. It was a question of money, naturally. He was into software too, but his company had gone bankrupt. I think most of these companies do. According to Natasha, half the time he either stayed in bed all day, or got up and played the clarinet.

Natasha told me more about her marriage than I wanted to know. Most people can't get it through their heads that their lives are not quite as fascinating as they think. Natasha rattled on and on. A lot of what she said had no relevance whatsoever. Certainly not to the issue of divorce. Under our no-fault law, nobody cares about your sex life.

I finally got rid of her. As she left, I saw Tommy sitting outside in the waiting room. I'm a solo practitioner—I don't have any partners—but my office is part of a suite of offices, and we share a common receptionist. The current one was named Helen, and common is an accurate way to describe her. She had recently given notice. She was thoroughly incompetent, so it hardly mattered.

Helen was sitting at her desk doing her nails. It was one of her favorite activities.

I motioned Tommy to come in, and he did. He seemed awkward and ill at ease. I pointed to a chair, and he sat down. I was face to face with Tommy Wingate, at last.

I looked closely at the man. I have to say, it irritated me somehow that he called himself Wingate. Didn't he have a name of his own? I felt like asking him, what was your maiden name, but somehow I thought he wouldn't get the joke.

This was my first chance to get a real look at Tommy. He had very regular features, an acceptable nose, and a kind of mildly square chin. He was good looking, in a counter-cultural sort of way. He wore his dark blonde hair in a ponytail; I had noticed that at Harriet's funeral. He had pale blue eyes, very pale, very blue; and he was clean-shaven, possibly for my benefit. He was wearing a plain white T-shirt, blue jeans, a denim jacket, and some kind of running shoes, maybe Nikes. There were no visible signs of a tattoo or of body piercing, except for a small gold earring in his left ear. He seemed uncomfortable, and kept shifting and fidgeting restlessly in the chair. He was one of these people whose knees were constantly in motion. In his hand, he was holding a large white envelope.

I shook his hand. "It's a pleasure to see you, Tommy."

He had a likeable though somewhat bashful smile. I had begun with a prejudice against him. The whole thing smelled bad—I mean, marrying an old woman, what was that all about? And then moving out, renting an apartment with a girlfriend, even, for God's sake, taking his girlfriend to his wife's funeral. I had no reason to feel friendly toward Tommy. In fact, one of my recurrent nightmares revolved around people like Tommy Wingate. I had this awful fear that one of my daughters would bring home a Tommy someday, like a cat bringing in a dead mouse, and present him as my future son-in-law, or, more likely, as a significant-other, or just somebody who was going to disappear with her into the bedroom and shut the door.

I was being unfair, I suppose. OK, Tommy didn't look like a bank president, or the kind of young person who wins the Westinghouse science award for discovering a better treatment for prostate cancer or a new subatomic particle. On the other hand, he didn't look malevolent. He had a kind of vacant look, and I had the feeling he would not do well on an intelligence test. But this was certainly no crime. He also didn't look like the boys my kids *actually* brought home or went to parties with. These guys were intelligent, I suppose—they had computers, took Advanced Placement Calculus, and their parents had dragged them to Europe, but they were also sullen and impenetrable. They were kids who wore size 50 blue jeans that stayed up over their visible polka dot underpants through some miracle of modern physics. They were kids whose only communication with my generation was a series of grunting noises, who came in packs, and who all disappeared immediately into some room or other with a loud slamming of the door. This was followed by a blast of hideous noise that they somehow defined as music, played at a decibel level that would turn anybody deaf.

I offered Tommy some coffee, but he said no thank you. He looked exceedingly nervous. I filled Tommy in on some of the probate details. I was handling the estate, I said, on behalf of the family. Barbara had asked me to do this. Of course, we thought at the time there was a will, and that the will named her as executor; but the will had disappeared, to our surprise. He had no idea what an executor was, so I explained it as best I could. "The executor takes care of the estate—you know, collects the property, pays the debts, handles things."

He nodded.

I went on: "There was another will, but let's skip it for now; I'll come back to that later," I said. "That one also disappeared."

He nodded again. Then I explained that if no will showed up, then Mrs. Wingate had died intestate, and the estate would be divided among members of the family. He, as the surviving husband, might get a share of the estate. I told him I wasn't sure exactly how much, it depended on certain things. But surely there would be something for him. The estate, as near as I could figure right now, was likely to run on the order of twenty million dollars.

Tommy said: "Wow."

I said, "There's a federal tax.... Though not on the portion that goes to a surviving spouse. That's you."

That brought out a second "wow." But he didn't register any really *strong* emotion—not surprise, not excitement. Just the same nervous blue-eyed stare.

"That's assuming... well, never mind," I said. I explained that he could speak to me about any problems or if he had any questions about the estate, what was going to happen, and anything along those lines.

He nodded again.

"Now," I said, "can we see the envelope?"

He handed it over. It was a plain white envelope, sealed. There was nothing on it but the name "Harriet Wingate," written in what I recognized as her handwriting. I reached for a letter-opener and slit it open. Inside was a single sheet of paper. It was handwritten. The paper was torn raggedly along the top—I would say about a third of it had been torn off.

The paper—God help us—was a will. It was what is called in California a holographic will, that is, a handwritten will. In California, if you write out a will by yourself, you don't need witnesses. This was one of those wills. It was short and sweet: "This is the last will of Harriet Wingate. I leave half my estate to my husband Tommy. I leave the other half in equal shares to my nieces Barbara Homans and Karen Bridges. It is my wish that Barbara should act as my executor." That was all. It was signed "Harriet Wingate." There were no witnesses. There was also no date. The date—if there was one—had been torn off.

"Can I see it?" he said.

I handed it to him, and he read it slowly. "Wow," he said. "This is Harriet's will."

"Well, yes, it's a will. We call this kind of will a holograph." I gave him the legal definition, and I repeated it. "You don't need witnesses, if you do it this way."

Again, nothing seemed to register. There was something very opaque, about Tommy, about the look in his eyes. I had no idea what he was thinking. I just couldn't fathom him. I guess I don't know many people like Tommy. Or people who I *think* are like Tommy.

In some ways, objectively speaking, he had very little going for him. Apparently he had no job. If he had much education, it certainly didn't show. Somehow I felt he had no family, or not much of one. Yet when I told him he was potentially a millionaire, it didn't seem to get past his vacant blue eyes. Nothing seemed to penetrate.

Was it that Tommy didn't care? Or was it that he had learned, somewhere or somehow, that it was better not to show what he was thinking, and what he was feeling? That it was safer that way? Was there something in his background so massively repressive, that it, well, made him what he was? I wished I knew more about his past.

I went on: "I want to thank you, Tommy, for bringing me this document, this... uh, will. It's really important. But there's something not quite kosher about it."

"Kosher?"

"Not quite right, I mean. For one thing, it's awfully short, just a couple of lines. Why did Harriet write this thing out? Why did she give it to you? She had another will, a long one, all legal and proper; I drew it up myself. It was, well, more detailed, to put it mildly."

He said nothing for a while. Then he said: "So this one is no good? The one I gave you?"

"I didn't say that. The will I drafted for her, the long one— that one disappeared. We can't find it anywhere."

"You looked for it?"

"Yes. In her house. In her safe deposit box."

"She kept things in the house," he said. "She had a desk, upstairs, you know?"

"We looked there," I said. "We looked everywhere. Barbara and I. Searched high and low. No, that will is absolutely gone. But there was another one...."

"Another will?" he said, repeating what I said as if he was trying to digest a tough piece of meat.

"Another will," I said. "But that one's gone too. We can't find it. So... maybe this one—the one in the envelope—*is* the only valid will."

"She said it was important," Tommy said. "She gave me this envelope, and she said it was important." He said: "I did what she told me to do."

"I'm sure you did.... There's something else," I said. "This will is torn: see? Somebody—maybe Harriet, maybe somebody else—tore off the top third of this piece of paper. Maybe there was something there—I imagine the date was there. But it's gone, torn off."

He said, "It wasn't me. I never opened this up."

"I didn't say you did, Tommy. I'm sure you're telling me the truth. Maybe Mrs. Wingate did it herself—I mean, tore off the top. Maybe she did it even before she sealed the envelope. But why would she do that? Why would she want to get rid of the date?"

Here I was thinking out loud. I was trying to remember the exact words of the California Probate Code on this particular subject, that is, a holographic will that had no date. Tommy obviously was not going to contribute to a discussion of the California Probate Code. Or any other discussion, I would imagine. "Tearing off the date.... What does that do? It doesn't make the will invalid; you don't *need* a date, not in California. But... with no date, we can't be sure if this is the *last* will, or whether some other will came later. Because we don't know when this one was written."

Tommy said nothing.

"I have to tell you, Tommy, that Mrs. Wingate—well, she did some peculiar things, in the last months, especially things that had to do with her will. Did she... ever discuss it with you, Tommy? Her will?"

He was very quiet, except for the fidgeting; and he shook his head. But I had a feeling, a hunch, an intuition, that he was telling a lie. Why I felt that way, I have no idea.

I said, "You're sure? I mean, you two were married. She didn't say anything about finances?"

"We didn't talk about money, no sir. Anyway, I wasn't living at the house. Not since... well, not for a while."

"You moved out, I know that. But, you said, you don't have a job. Could I ask you: where are you getting the money? I mean, how are you paying the rent?"

"I had some money... from Harriet. And, well, my girl-friend, she works."

His *wife* gave him money for rent, and his *girlfriend*, who he's living with, works. I mean, is this crazy or what? Another case where my friends in the East would say: typical California.

Tommy added, "I'm looking for a job. I had one before, but I got laid off."

"Your... friend: could you tell me her name?"

"Her name is Sophie."

"Have you... known her long?"

"Man, I don't know. Why are you asking me?"

Why indeed. I didn't have a good explanation. I switched the subject. "Don't be offended, Tommy, but I have to ask certain questions. You know, legal reasons. Were you on good terms? with Mrs. Wingate? You weren't living there, you said. Did you have some sort of argument, you and Mrs. Wingate? Was that why you moved out?"

He looked at me, with those water-blue eyes. I just couldn't read him. He seemed... blank. Slowly, he shook his head. "Argument? No way. We always got along," he said. "Me and Harriet. She was my friend. I used to visit her, at the house. Lots of times. We never argued. Never."

"I see."

"I mean it. We were... like that," he said, crossing his two fingers. I nodded my head. I guess I didn't convince him of my sincerity. For the first time, I sensed some emotion, some feeling in his voice. "You didn't know Harriet," he said. "She was awesome. She was terrific. She was really good to me. Most of my life, people treated me like garbage. Not Harriet."

There was a ring of honesty in this. Tommy really seemed to mean what he was saying. Maybe Harriet Wingate was a sort of mother figure for him. Or grandmother figure. Who knows. He said she was awesome. He said I didn't know her. Well, he was wrong about that. I knew her... well, slightly, anyway. She was a nice old woman, and a strong woman, a woman with definite opinions. A forceful character. But awesome?

He also said they were "friends." That's not what husbands usually call their wives. Or maybe it is. Most wives, I hope, are more than a friend.

I'm not just thinking about sex. That's there, of course. You don't have sex with friends. Or maybe you do. God knows what young people are up to these days. Some of them would have sex with a vacuum cleaner, if they could. Or is this just my imagination?

Sex... between Tommy and Harriet Wingate? A young guy like Tommy, and a woman past 80.... I couldn't even start to picture it. Or was I just being ageist? The AARP would never forgive me. They are constantly bombarding us with propaganda which seems to imply that senior citizens are like everybody else: they love sex, they have sex all the time, with or without Viagra, and so on. To read some of these articles, you would think nursing homes were seething hotbeds of lust.

Of course, I wasn't going to pry into Tommy's sex life or his relationship with Harriet Wingate. I did want to worm a bit more information out of him. Lawyers like me have that privilege: we can ask embarrassing questions, if we have a good legal excuse, or at least *claim* to have a good legal excuse. And we can always make one up. The clients have no way of knowing if it's right or wrong.

"I have to ask you some things, Tommy," I said, bumbling a bit, "I mean, I have to get some of the facts down straight. It's about... handling the estate, you see. There's a lot of money involved."

He nodded his head. I plunged ahead: "And... your status... as the putative husband, you see."

He stared at me. "Putative" was clearly not in his vocabulary, but I saw no reason to give him definitions. I went on: "I need to ask you... about your marriage...."

"Huh?"

"Well... it's kind of an unusual marriage. You know, you were a lot younger than Mrs. Wingate... and, well, because of the will and that sort of thing, your rights... as a husband, you understand...."

He didn't understand. I don't blame him, considering the nonsense I was blathering. He said, "I don't understand.... Like, what's the question?"

What, indeed. "Well, this is embarrassing, but... well, do you have proof? I mean, of your marriage. A marriage certificate? Can you tell me *when* you got married... and where?"

"Vegas," he said.

"Vegas?"

"We drove to Vegas. I drove, Harriet was in the car, you know? We drove at night. There's a certificate, I got it someplace, or maybe it's in Harriet's house. It was all, like, legal. Listen: if somebody wants to say we weren't really married...."

"I'm not saying that. Nobody's saying that, I think. I just... had to ask, for, uh, legal aspects."

"We got married. Right there in Vegas. One of those little chapels, you know? We had witnesses and everything. We even bought a ring and stuff."

He seemed upset by the question, and he went on: "Flowers, too. Man, it was a big bouquet. We got it at an all-night supermarket. And a regular minister, he was there. At the wedding. I saw his license, he had it framed, it was on the wall. His wife, she was one of the witnesses. I don't remember who the other one was. Somebody who worked there, I think. It was legal and all."

I wondered what the minister thought of this unlikely couple. I suppose he had seen stranger things. Well, not much stranger. But who knows? Anything is possible in Las Vegas. It's a human zoo. I suppose too that as long as you paid your money, the minister didn't care very much. He would marry two chimpanzees, if they paid the fee. Or one human and one chimpanzee, for that matter.

I wondered if Tommy kissed the bride after the ceremony; after the minister said, I pronounce you husband and wife. I couldn't picture this either. But I kept my mouth shut. "Do you remember the date?"

"Like, it was a year ago... more than that, maybe. No, I don't remember exactly. It was summer, July maybe, last year. I mean, I could check it."

I didn't feel like telling Tommy most married people remember the date they were married, so that they can celebrate their anniversary. I certainly remember mine: May 17th. Celia would be terribly hurt if I forgot that date. And I never do forget. I always get her something. Flowers at least. She doesn't forget me, either.

There was an awkward silence. This line of questioning obviously bothered Tommy, because he suddenly said: "They got to keep records, don't they? Those ministers. You could find out, couldn't you? The date and stuff."

"Absolutely," I said, "I wouldn't worry."

He seemed relieved. The marriage seemed stranger than ever. It didn't seem like a marriage at all. Occasionally you do read in the paper about a June and December romance where some guy of 25 marries an old granny. It's odd enough to get in the papers. Of course, such a guy *never* looks like Tommy. But those are real, if peculiar, marriages. Maybe they even have sex. Tommy's marriage seemed... hollow: it was some sort of charade.

But in a way, that made it *less* strange. Less strange, insofar as it didn't seem like a real marriage. It was some kind of arrangement—something that left Tommy free to conduct his sex life, for example, as if there was no marriage. But then why marry? Why did they drive two hundred miles or three hundred miles or whatever it was to Las Vegas, and go through with this charade? What was the point of it all?

Was it the money? Was he after her money? But Tommy, whatever his failings, did not strike me as a gigolo. Frankly, he didn't seem bright enough or twisted enough to marry an old lady for her money. You had to scheme and plot and manipulate; you had to lie and pretend and act a part. That was simply not my impression of Tommy. He seemed... authentic to me, in some peculiar way. What you saw was what you got.

But what on earth did Harriet Wingate see? He was young, he was good-looking, he had a ponytail: but what could all that possibly mean to her?

Or was I selling her short? Was this an example of ageism again? Maybe she fell in love with Tommy. Her last chance for romance. A lonely old woman, and a rather dim, harmless young man.... Maybe it was Harriet's idea, after all. Maybe she did it to give him a share of the estate; a share nobody could possibly contest. That made at least a little bit of sense. Could that be it?

And Tommy? What about him? Was it his last chance... but if so, for what?

"One more thing," I said. "You're going to think this is a crazy question, but I'll explain it...."

"OK."

"I have to ask you: Did your wife, Mrs. Wingate... did she have any cats?"

"Cats?"

"Yes. Cats."

He stared at me again. "Cats?"

That was twice he said "cats." I nodded my head. "Cats. You know. Pet cats." I was tempted to add: c-a-t.

He shook his head, vigorously. "Man, that's a funny question. Harriet, she hated cats. She was allergic to cats. She had these terrific allergies, you know? She used to break out, you know, get a rash; she couldn't even get near a cat."

"So she never had a cat."

"I told you, no. No cats. She told me, once she had this cleaning lady, I can't remember her name, this was before she had Edna, anyway, this cleaning lady used to have a cat, the cleaning lady did. I mean, just having a cat, when she came over, maybe there was hair or stuff on her clothes, you know? Harriet would get this rash, so she had to get rid of this woman, get another one, that's when she hired Edna...."

"Did she know anybody who had cats? Besides this cleaning lady?"

He shook his head again, no.

I went on: "Do the names Teddy, Beulah and Katie mean anything to you?"

"Teddy, Beulah and Katie?"

"Yes: do those names ring a bell?"

He scratched his head, and thought for a while. I could almost see the gears moving and whirring in his brain. He said: "I used to know a guy named Teddy," he said. "He lived in my town. Teddy something. Big guy. He had a scar on his nose... Beulah, Beulah. What kind of a name is Beulah?"

"Just a name."

"No, I never knew nobody named Beulah. Katie: let me see. No, I don't know no Katie. Who are these people?"

"They're not people," I said. "They're cats. They're supposed to be the names of Mrs. Wingate's cats."

"Man, that's the craziest thing I ever heard. I told you, she couldn't, like, even be in a room with a cat."

I told him the story. I told him about Peter Elver, and the cat will. He rolled his eyes. He said, hey, that had to be a mistake. That lawyer, he must be nuts. It couldn't be Harriet, he said. Cats! Crazy, he said. Unless he was a terrific actor, and I doubt that very much, the cat will was a complete surprise. At least he confirmed what Barbara had said about Mrs. Wingate and her relationship, or non-relationship, to *felis domesticus*.

Curiouser and curiouser, as they say in Alice in Wonderland. Curiouser and curiouser, all the time.

I told Tommy I might have more questions and that the estate was, well, complicated; did he need any money, by way of an advance, from the estate? He shook his head and said no he didn't, and then muttered something about trying to get a job, and he was OK for now. The money really didn't seem to loom large in his mind. Or maybe he was just playing it cool.

I had formed a definite opinion about Tommy. I can't say I liked him, but I found him somehow harmless and even appealing. But, you know, I'm not Sherlock Holmes. I don't have the instincts these great detectives have. I'm certainly not infallible. In fact, I'm wrong most of the time, or at least it seems that way. For all I knew, this dumb quiet guy with the pale blue eyes, might be a seething inferno inside—an ax murderer, a serial killer, a savage rapist or whatever.

Or somebody who smothered old ladies with the handiest, nearest pillow?

I was sorry Barbara had ever planted that seed in my mind. I kept telling myself, Harriet Wingate died a natural death. But I couldn't quite convince myself, to tell the truth.

9

It was long after Tommy had gone when I was sitting in my office, doodling and trying to think clearly, that I had a brilliant flash of insight. I thought: maybe I'm not so bad at this game as I imagine. You see, it suddenly dawned on me what Harriet Wingate meant, when she named three nonexistent cats Teddy, Beulah, and Katie. I think it was the doodling that did the trick. I was writing these three names, over and over. Then I wrote the initials very large, and the key to the mystery jumped right out at me.

I guess I was thinking at the same time about the torn holographic will. I remembered that it left everything to Tommy, Barbara, and Karen. Tommy, Barbara, and Karen. Another set of three whose names started with T, B, and K. That couldn't be a coincidence. She must have picked those three names in the cat will quite deliberately—she must have meant some kind of signal or code. But who she was signaling to, and *why* was she sending these signals? That part was still completely lost on me.

In any event, I now had *three* wills on my mind. Two of them, to be sure, were lost and gone. A third one, short and sweet, was in my hands, but it lacked a date and was torn in a funny way. I had expected Harriet Wingate's estate to be easy money. Now, possibly, it was going to be a terrific headache. *If* I was going to end up handling it at all. Which was by no means a sure thing.

And to make matters worse, the fourth will—or rather, evidence *about* a fourth will—showed up the very next day.

Like everything else concerning the estate of Harriet Wingate, the fourth will was totally unexpected. I was in my office working when Helen, the receptionist, took time out from reading *Cosmopolitan* to come into my office to tell me there was someone to see me.

It was about eleven o'clock in the morning, a brilliant morning, very California, all sunshine and glow. The fog had burned off by mid-morning, and a wonderful brightness came in through my window. I had seen clients until 10:30, and was now puzzling over one of my files which concerned a lawsuit against my Armenian restaurant owner. A personal injury case: one of his customers, a middle-aged woman, had slipped on some pilaf, which was on the floor instead of on the plate where it belonged. She landed with a thud on her bottom, damaging this and that to the extent of a million dollars, if you believed her story, which I most certainly did not.

I don't handle this kind of case—I don't do personal injury work, as a rule. But the defendant was my client, and I keep my eye on what's happening, monitor the case, and give him the benefit of my advice, for what it's worth. Actually, it's not worth very much.

I didn't have any appointments, so I was surprised when Helen said I had somebody waiting to see me. "Who is it?" I asked. "I don't have anybody listed."

She shrugged her shoulders. "No idea."

I don't expect her to *care* about my work, but I wish she could at least *pretend*. I asked: "Man or woman?"

"Man. Young," she said.

"Well, send him in."

I don't advertise, as some lawyers do, and I very, very rarely get a client who just walks in off the streets. But of course this can happen, I suppose. I adjusted my tie.

My visitor was young: about twenty, I would say. He was very tall and gangly, loose jointed, and he had a narrow, pleasant face, bright brown eyes, and straight black hair slicked over his forehead. He looked very normal, very collegiate in fact: he was the very picture of a student, which in fact he was. Like Tommy, though, he had an earring: a small gold earring in his right ear. Is that standard these days? He wore chino pants, and a denim jacket which said: "University of California." I gathered that referred to Berkeley. He was carrying a backpack. It looked heavy, as if it was full of books, as if he had dropped in to see me between Calculus and French 101.

"My name is Joe Pangea," he said. "P-A-N-G-E-A. Three syllables. Lots of people mispronounce it. I hope I'm not disturbing you. I should have called first."

"It's OK."

"I *was* going to call. But I thought, what I have to say, well, it'll just sound goofy. It's better to talk to you in person. I was down here, in this area, anyway: I have a friend in San Carlos, I'm having dinner with him. He's a student at Cal. I am too; we were studying together. I don't have classes today.... Anyway, I thought... well, here I am. Do you have some time?"

"Maybe. Depends what this is all about."

"Well, it's a pretty strange story."

"A lot of people tell me strange stories," I said. "Go right ahead." Strange story: these were magic words; my curiosity took over immediately. "OK," he said. "I believe you represent the estate of Harriet Wingate."

"Yes. Anyway, let's say I do." Harriet Wingate's estate: it was the last thing I expected. How on earth was this college kid connected to Harriet Wingate? "Why do you ask? You have some business with the estate?"

"Not exactly," he said. "Well, actually, yes. I better explain myself. You see... Harriet Wingate, she was my grandmother."

"Your grandmother?" I was astonished. It was news to me. Harriet, I always thought, had no living descendants. Of any type. She never said a word about such a thing. Harriet had no children. I mean, I always *thought* she had no children. "She... was your grandmother? Are you sure?"

"Yes, I'm sure," Joe said. "But I don't blame you for acting surprised. I expected that. It wasn't exactly a well-known fact. I never knew it myself until recently. Mr. May, I think I better tell you the whole story."

After the famous cat will, I suppose nothing about the Wingate estate should have surprised me. A newly hatched grandson was in a way par for the course.

"And," he added, "there's something else. My grandmother gave me something... to give you." He reached into his backpack and took out a large manila envelope. "But first I better tell you how... well, how I came to have this in my possession."

"Go ahead."

"Sure. I'm a student at Berkeley," he said. "I have to tell you, I never actually met Mrs. Wingate. My family lives in Chicago. Well, not really in Chicago, in a suburb of Chicago, River Forest. I always knew I was adopted, I knew that the man I called my dad, Henry Pangea, wasn't my real father. But he's the only father I've ever known. He married my mom when I was less than a year old. So... well, you understand. He's a great guy, my dad. I'm not one of those adopted kids that gets an itch to find their biological parents, to find out who they really are. I mean, I know who I really am. What difference does it make, the biology part, you know, a few sperm cells. My dad, my mom's husband, he's been good to me. He's been the best father a guy could have; we're very close.

"So anyway: I never really had this urge to find my biological dad. But you know, you can't help wondering, you can't help thinking, what really happened? My mom always told me my father was killed in an auto accident just after I was born. When I was a little kid I believed her. You always believe everything your mom tells you. But when I was in high school, I started to doubt it. There was something fishy about the story. For God's sake, she never even told me his *name*; and if I brought the subject up, she got upset. It was obviously a painful subject, and I realized quickly, it's better if I don't say anything. More and more, I got curious; there was some sort of secret there, I knew that, and I guess it was just... well, let's just say: curiosity."

I certainly know that feeling. Anyway, he continued:

"I have to tell you, too, that my mom isn't well; she's not old, she's only in her late 40's, but she's got a heart condition, so we kind of treat her with kid gloves. The three of us. I have two sisters, younger sisters; well, half-sisters, really, but that's never really made any difference.

"So OK, when I was 16, 17, I guess I bugged my mother enough so she decided she had to tell me something. You know, she used to say, when I asked about my real dad, *this* is your real dad, he raised you from a baby. She meant my adoptive father, and of course she was right. He was the one who played soccer with me and helped me with my homework and whatever. But I said, mom, I know that, and I'll always love him and he'll always be my dad, but can't you understand what I'm asking? You know, I said to her once, I just don't believe this story about the auto accident. Maybe you don't even know who my father *was*. Well, she got flustered. I shouldn't have said that. She said, of course I do.

"OK then, I said, maybe you weren't ever married to this guy, maybe I was illegitimate. And you know what, mom, I don't care. It's not a disgrace, for God's sake. Not in this day and age.

"She started to cry, and I felt ashamed of myself. But then she said: you're right, I should tell you the truth. I hate lying to you, I love you too much. Your father's name was Gregory. Gregory Hendricks. And no, we weren't married, Gregory and I. I was young and stupid, and he... well, never mind. Anyway, he deserted me as soon as he knew I was pregnant. He came around again, a few times, after you were born, but Henry— your dad—was already going with me, and he told him to get out and stay out, don't bother us, and I never saw him again. Joe, she said, this may be a hard thing to say to you, but I should never have gotten mixed up with him. Your father, your biological father, he was plain no good. He was good-looking, flashy, he had a kind of charm, but he was also violent and abusive, she said. Later on, he even went to prison.... I asked, what for? What did he do? She said she didn't know.

"Well, at least now I knew his name. Gregory Hendricks. I asked my mom, what kind of people are they, where do they live? The Hendricks family. She said, I don't know. Anyway, he wasn't really a Hendricks, she said. They adopted him. His real mother wasn't married either, and she put him up for adoption. Gregory was a disaster from the start. I think the Hendrickses finally washed their hands of him.

"And the mother? I asked. My grandmother? What about her? Well, I never met her, my mom said. But I know who she is, because Gregory knew, and he used to tell me about her, though I think he never got to see her. But he would talk about her, sort of by way of bragging. She was rich, he said, a rich woman, and she lived in California, in the Bay Area. And, I asked, is she still alive? My mom said, I don't know, she'd be fairly old; but yes, she could be still alive. And where's this Hendricks guy now, still in prison? I asked. I was careful not to say: my father. She said: I don't know. I heard he was dead.

"I didn't ask anything more. Then, when I was going to go to college, I applied to a lot of places, but I really wanted to go to Berkeley. I heard a lot about it, and that was my first choice. I had good grades, good SAT's, and I was accepted there. I was excited about it, and a couple of my friends were going too, they also got in, but I could see mom didn't want me to go. My dad did, he was as excited as I was, but mom was reluctant. It's a great school, mom, I told her, it's really hard to get in: you should be proud of me. She said, I am proud of you. But it's so far away, and I'll miss you. Nowadays, with jets and all, that's nothing, I said. Then I realized, she was holding something back. I think it was because of... the rich old lady. Is it because of my grandmother? I asked.

"She had to admit that it was. She found out, I'm not sure how, maybe after our conversation she started doing some looking around. Anyway, she knew that my grandmother was still alive, still living in the Bay Area. This was Harriet Wingate, of course. My mom never got in touch with her though, and she was deathly afraid I'd want to go see her. But I promised I wouldn't. I swore it to my mom.

"So I went off to Berkeley, and studied, and all that sort of thing, and the first year went by. I'm a sophomore now. I love it there. I'm going to be in a fraternity. My grades are pretty good, too. And I guess my mom thought I was growing up, getting mature enough to handle things. So she said to me, during the summer break: Joe, if you want to, you can get in touch with Harriet Wingate. She's your grandmother, after all.

She's not responsible for what her son did, and she hasn't got any other children or grandchildren, you're the only one, and she doesn't even know you exist. Would she *want* to see me, I asked? But of course, my mom didn't know the answer to that question. So I said, I'll think about it, mom.

"I wasn't sure what to do, or whether to do anything. Oh, I was curious… a real grandmother. My mom's parents were dead, and my dad's parents, I mean my adoptive dad, they died when I was little. So I really wanted to see my grandmother. But I could tell the whole thing was going to be ticklish for everybody concerned. Finally, I decided I wasn't going to go see Harriet Wingate, you know, burst in on her and say, hello there, I'm your grandson, you don't know I exist. I decided not to call her on the phone either. That would be just as bad, and I didn't want her to hang up on me or something like that. So I wrote her a long letter instead.

"I told her my story, and I said in the letter, I could understand it if she didn't want to see me, or talk to me or have anything to do with me, and I would respect her decision, and she'd never hear from me again. But if she wanted to, I'd like to meet her sometime."

"Did she answer?"

"She did. I had left a phone number where she could reach me, and an email address. But she wrote a letter instead…."

"Do you have the letter?"

"She told me, when she wrote to me, to destroy the letter. She said this was important. So I did."

"Did she say *why* she wanted you to destroy the letter?"

He said: "Not exactly. Maybe… well, the embarrassment of this illegitimate grandchild, but maybe it was something else…. Let me finish telling you, about the letter."

"Go on."

"She said she was glad to hear from me, and that she would like to meet me someday. She said, you sound like a fine young man, I know they only take the best at Berkeley, and I'm glad you turned out so well. Your mother should be proud of you. But, she said, it's not possible for us to get together now. Under no circumstances should I make any attempt to see her or contact her. She said she couldn't explain, but it was a matter of life and death...."

"Life and death?!"

"She said, if anybody knew that I even existed, a tragedy might occur. That's the very word she used: a tragedy."

I had a sudden thought: "Did she say anything in her letter about... her family here? About her husband?"

"Husband? I didn't know she had one."

"She did."

He seemed puzzled. "No, she didn't mention a husband."

"Did she say anything about her son? Your father? Whether he was dead or alive?"

"No, nothing. They said, I mean mom said she thought he was dead. I suppose Mrs. Wingate knew that too."

"I was just curious," I said. "By the way, yes, there is definitely a husband. But go on, Joe."

"Well, I found this letter pretty weird, as you can imagine. I wanted to go see her anyway, no matter what she said. I've got a car, an old beat-up one, I could just drive down here. But I thought to myself, she has her reasons, and I have no right to interfere with her life. So I accepted what she said. I tried to put her out of my mind, and I did. I've got a pretty tough schedule, I'm an econ major, and I'm thinking of law school. I've got to get the grades, and... well, I have a social life too. So I wasn't spending every day brooding about my grandmother. I let things go, I wasn't sure what to do, probably nothing.... I didn't tell my folks about the letter. Anyway, about a month ago, I heard from her again."

"From Harriet Wingate?"

"Yes. Again by mail. I got this thick envelope. Certified mail, I had to sign for it. Inside was a short letter, and a sealed envelope. The letter said, Joe, I'm trusting you not to open this envelope. If anything happens to me, please take it to Frank May. He's an attorney, in San Mateo. He will be handling my estate. Give it to him. Naturally, I thought that was pretty weird. But I felt honor-bound to do what she said. I thought, I'll wait for another message. I had a feeling she would want to see me... soon."

"But you didn't get any message."

"No, I didn't."

"So you never actually met her."

He seemed to hesitate—was this just regret, about the lost opportunity? He said, "No, I never met her...."

"I'm sorry," I said. "She was quite a person."

He nodded. "I'm sorry too. Sorry that I'll never know her. But... the least I can do is follow her instructions. So: here I am, Mr. May."

"Call me Frank. Why did you wait until now?"

"I didn't know she was dead. That's another funny thing. A couple of days ago, I had a message on my voicemail. It said, 'This is a message for Joe Pangea. Harriet Wingate has passed away.' The guy who called—it was a man—didn't leave a name or a number. I had an econ quiz the next day, so I didn't do anything. Then I looked you up and here I am."

"You have no idea who it was? The telephone caller?"

"None at all."

"Was it somebody old, young, or what? Anything funny about the voice?"

"I would say: not particularly young. But I can't be sure. Nothing funny about the voice, no accent or anything. If I had to guess, I would say an educated person. But the message was so short, I can't be sure."

"Do you have the document?"

"I do." He took an envelope out of his back pack. It was a plain white envelope, no markings or words on it. It was sealed.

I opened it up with a sinking feeling. I knew immediately it was going to be a will. What else? Everybody who comes to see me brings me another one of Harriet Wingate's wills. The woman positively sprouted wills.

I wasn't completely wrong. Not that there was an actual will inside the envelope; instead there was a copy of a will—a xerox of a will. The will itself was short—a two page holograph. It was in Harriet Wingate's handwriting—at any rate, it was in a handwriting that looked like hers. It was in good form for a holograph; maybe she copied it from some sort of form book. The text was simple: it left $75,000 "to my grandson, Joe Pangea," various small gifts to friends, relatives, and to charities (none of them had anything to do with cats). And the rest of the estate, one-half to Tommy Wingate, one-half to be divided between Barbara and Karen. It appointed Barbara Homans executor, to serve without bond. It was very similar, in other words, to the will I had drawn up; it was missing many of the technical provisions, but they hardly matter.

There was also a note, and it was addressed to me: "Frank. This is my will. You will find the original in my home; Barbara knows where I keep it. Thank you. Harriet Wingate."

From the evidence of the copy, from the date on it, this was the most recent will of all—it was written a week or so before Harriet died. Well, the most recent as far as I knew. There could be a dozen other wills. And there was no date on the holograph Tommy had given to me. Possibly that was the most recent will. I say, possibly. I doubted it, of course.

This was, as I said, only a photocopy. Where was the original? A good question. Needless to say, we had never come across it when we searched through the house. It was certainly not in the drawer where Harriet kept her papers. Nor did we find it in the safe deposit box. It was gone, in other words. Harriet Wingate, of course, could have destroyed it. Or somebody else. But the note said I would find the original, and Barbara would know where it was. Whatever could that mean? Barbara had said nothing about this will, and I had gotten no instructions whatsoever.

So now we had three missing wills and one torn holograph. Terrific.

I told Joe Pangea that the document was a will, or rather a copy of a will. He was surprised, or acted surprised, when I told him that the document left him a gift of $75,000. "That was very generous," he said, "I never met her, as I told you."

"I've got to tell you, Joe, don't get your hopes up. We don't have the original, it's lost. And without that, this is just another piece of paper."

If the original will did not turn up—and there's no reason to think it would—would he have a claim on his grandmother's estate? Biologically speaking, he was her closest relative. But he had been adopted, and that usually severs blood relationships. Nonetheless, the legal situation was somewhat more complicated than that. He might have a claim, in some states, if, for instance, she didn't know he existed because of some mistake; but of course she did know he existed, so that line of argument was out.

In any event, I explained, since his father had been adopted, since he, Joe, was also adopted, then he had no inheritance rights with respect to blood relatives, that is, no claim on his grandmother's estate. The Probate Code of California makes that clear. (At least that's the way I remembered the Code. I made a mental note to check this out later on.)

"My folks are pretty comfortable," he said. "I wasn't really looking for money."

What were you looking for? I wondered; and as if he heard me, he said, "I was looking for... a grandmother. Like I said, my mom's parents are dead, and she really doesn't have any family. My dad's parents are dead too. He has brothers and sisters, but they're all in Florida, and he has an aunt there, too, but to tell you the truth, I never really liked them much. Anyway, I was looking for somebody who knew something about my background, about the part that was so mysterious. I was looking for my father, I guess, even though I said I wasn't. I thought my grandmother could help me.... I've always felt like, well, like somebody with a big fat secret hanging over their head, and I thought I might find out some answers. But it's never going to be."

I said, "Well, Joe, it's true, your grandmother passed away and we can't do anything about that. I'm sorry you never had a chance to see her. But you've got other relatives here."

"Relatives?"

"Mrs. Wingate had family. Two nieces in particular; very fine women. They're cousins of yours. They live near here. This woman Barbara, the woman she named as executor, she's one of the nieces. You might want to meet them."

"I might," he said, "but it's not the same."

I didn't have the heart to tell him that maybe somebody had, shall we say, helped his grandmother along to the grave. I know I was skeptical when Barbara brought this up, but I was beginning to feel it was a distinct possibility. There were certainly a lot of strange things going on. Harriet Wingate had been afraid of something or somebody. That was clear. And why did she execute four different wills? Something was rotten, not in the state of Denmark, but in Santa Clara and San Mateo counties, California, USA.

I also didn't have the heart to tell Joe that his new-found cousins were not likely to be overjoyed at meeting him. I don't think they would be keen on the idea of a grandson. And an illegitimate one at that. Karen especially. Imagine, an illegitimate child in the family tree of her beloved Spively's.

10

I felt I had to call Barbara and give her a full report. She was as surprised as I was to learn about Joe Pangea: "Frank, I'm in shock. I heard vague rumors once, years ago. About Aunt Harriet. But I put them out of my mind. Do you think this Joe person is telling the truth?"

"I think so. We can certainly check out his story, if we have to."

She said: "I suppose he's after her money."

"I don't know," I said. "He made a good impression on me."

"Everybody makes a good impression on you, Frank," she said, her voice dripping with sarcasm.

"Barbara, that not even true. I'm a lawyer. I'm naturally cynical and suspicious."

"You're as cynical and suspicious as a stuffed teddy bear," she said. "For example, tell me exactly what you thought about Tommy. I happen to know he came to see you."

I said, "I'd rather not say."

"Naturally. I can just imagine. He seemed all... innocent. He's stupid, I'll grant you that. He's as dumb as they come. But dumb is not the same as innocent. What kind of a man would prey on an old lady, the way he did?"

"Barbara, I don't want to argue. 'Prey on' is pretty strong language. I admit, it's an odd situation. But do you have some evidence?"

"You're as bad as Karen. Evidence, indeed! What is this, a trial? I know what I know," she said, and hung up the phone.

I didn't like the ways things were going. Barbara seemed angry. An angry client is not a good idea. I had a vague fear about the future. The estate of Harriet Wingate seemed likely to bring me grief instead of money. In any case, I needed to get back in Barbara's good graces. I called her up the next day and flagellated myself (metaphorically speaking) on the telephone. She seemed mollified.

"You'll see, Frank, that I'm not always wrong," she said. "I'm doing a little checking on my own."

"About Joe Pangea?"

"No, something else."

"Could you give me a hint?"

"I'll tell you in good time."

I also brought up the matter of the Pangea will, or will number four, or whatever we wanted to call it. "The original is missing, of course," I said. "I just want to make 100% sure. *I* certainly never saw it, and I'm positive you didn't."

"Absolutely not. We went over everything, every scrap of paper, remember?"

"Right. We did. But Barbara, about this other business: don't hide things from me. You say you're 'checking.' Exactly what are you talking about?"

"You'll have to be patient, Frank."

But I didn't have to be patient. Or at least not *very* patient. She called me a few days later and asked to come see me. I said, sure, any time. She came to the office and sat down across from me with a determined look and a kind of gleam in her eye.

"You look like the cat who swallowed the canary," I said.

"I think I have some important information," she said.

"Great. Let's have it."

"I was going over some of my aunt's papers. Her check books, bank accounts, and so on. They go back for years. We were looking for wills, and so we just passed these things by, but of course they're important. Aunt Harriet never threw anything away; she kept all her records, and they're in terrific shape. Very neat and orderly. Well, that's no surprise. But I found some very, very strange things."

"Such as what?"

"Such as this: about five or six years ago, my aunt hired a private detective. Excuse me, 'private investigators' is what they call themselves now. She paid a lot of money. Maybe $20,000 all told, maybe more."

"For what purpose?"

"That's the mystery. I don't know. I looked up the firm, they're still in business. They advertise in the Yellow Pages and they have a website. They locate missing persons, they find 'deadbeat parents,' they find 'lost loved ones,' they do background checks—I'm quoting all this from their website. They promise discretion and confidentiality and so on. I called them, told them who I was, said I was the executor of the estate of Harriet Wingate, and I needed this information, but I got exactly nowhere."

"They wouldn't tell you."

"Not a word. Only the client can release that information, and that sort of thing. Well, the client is dead, I said, and I have to know. But they wouldn't say anything. I got nothing at all out of them."

"And what do *you* think, Barbara? You must have an idea."

"I do. I think she was looking for her son. And maybe for her grandson."

"Then I guess she didn't find them... If Joe is telling the truth, Barbara."

"I suppose... After all, this firm does specialize in missing persons, so that's a good guess. Why else would she be paying this money?"

"No idea."

"Anyway. That's not the main point. It's interesting that she hired these detectives, but, as I said, at least we can guess what the reason was. But I found out something else, something even more surprising. Somebody was blackmailing my aunt."

"Blackmailing her?"

"She was paying money every month, for the last year and half of her life: big money, $10,000 a month, to some company.... The name was Anguilla Inc. But there is no such company. I checked around, trying to find out something about this company. And I found out, it's nothing."

"What do you mean, it's nothing."

"It's a bank account. Nothing more. There's no such business; it's a dummy, a shell."

"And who was behind it, this shell?"

"I wish I knew. I don't."

"And do you have any idea—I guess you don't—*why* she was paying out this money?"

"Not a clue. I'm not even sure it was blackmail. Only what else could it be? Why else would she be paying that kind of money, month after month?"

"And how long did this continue?"

"Right up to the time she died. Something is fishy here, Frank. All these wills, the private detective, the payments...." I had to agree. We could raise a lot of questions, but we couldn't answer any of them. There was obviously more to the affairs of Harriet Wingate than met the eye. A lot more, probably.

11

That was only the beginning. Barbara, it seemed, had become a positive whirlwind of activity. When she made up her mind to take action, she could be a very determined woman. What all the activity was about, I wasn't quite sure. Anyway, it wouldn't surprise me to learn that *she* had hired a private detective. (Actually, as I found out later, she had.)

I didn't hear a word from her for a few days. They were busy days for me, and I didn't miss the entanglements of the Wingate estate. Then, after this brief lull, Barbara called me on the phone. Well, tried to call me. I was in my office talking to a client, so Helen took the message. Or messages. Barbara called twice in half an hour.

She said it was urgent. She *really* wanted me to call back, and as soon as I possibly could, which I did.

"Hi Barbara," I said, "where's the fire?"

She ignored this. "Frank, I want you to meet somebody."

"I'm always glad to meet somebody. Is this a potential client?"

"Be serious, Frank. This is important. I have some information... well, I think it sheds light on Aunt Harriet's death. Can you come over tonight?"

I hate to work at night or to do anything at night related to work. Celia doesn't like it either. It's one thing to bring home a briefcase from the office: that's standard procedure. I bring it home every night. About once a week I actually open the briefcase. Celia also brings home work. So, once in a while we're both working at home in the evening, but together, if you know what I mean. In the same house. Visiting clients, or going back to the office at night: that's another story. She doesn't like it and neither do I.

Still, I felt an obligation to Barbara. Celia knows I don't abuse my privileges. Not often, anyway. Besides, as you already know, I was curious. What was this all about?

We ate dinner and then I went off. I arrived at Barbara's condo at about eight o'clock.

She lived in downtown Palo Alto, a few blocks from University Avenue, which is basically the city's Main Street. Barbara lived in one of the nicer new developments. Palo Alto is terribly pricey. Too many billionaires live within the city limits, and they spoil things for ordinary human beings. Barbara's condo was close enough to downtown for her to walk to University Avenue—in case she had a passion for overpriced cappuccino, expensive foreign restaurants, rug stores perpetually going out of business, brokerage houses, and other amenities.

I rang, and Barbara answered the door. "Frank, it's good of you to come," she said. She had a coffee pot, coffee cups, and silverware on a tray in her living room, with a tempting mound of pastries beside these. When I entered, I saw her sister, Karen, and an unidentified but dignified man, gray at the temples, about fifty I would say.

Karen was a younger, smaller, and thinner version of her sister. I've known her for a number of years, though not as well as Barbara. She was divorced and had a daughter who lives in the East, Cincinnati or someplace. A married daughter, I think. Karen's main interest in life, as I may have mentioned, seemed to be family history. That's what she talked about incessantly. Maybe she had other interests: I'm just not aware of them. For all I know, she might be into origami or golf or politics. Probably not bowling.

We said hello to each other. She was drinking a cup of coffee and nibbling on one of the pastries. She looked... tense, if you know what I mean. There was something in the air—an argument, I would guess.

Barbara had a kind of grim smile on her face. She said, "Frank, this is Dr. Arthur Swanson. He was Aunt Harriet's doctor for many years."

Dr. Swanson nodded his head, solemnly, no doubt to confirm this earth-shaking fact. He said, "Yes, I was her primary care physician. I'm with the Palo Alto clinic. My actual specialty is arthritis, and Mrs. Wingate had a rather mild case of it. But in any event, I was what you might call her family doctor, her general doctor. Oh, I knew Harriet forever. In fact, Joseph Wingate was a dear friend of mine."

For a moment I didn't connect. "Joseph Wingate?"

"Her late husband. In any event, I've also known Barbara and Karen for years. Well, I'll get to the point. Barbara asked me to come here tonight. About a year ago Harriet called me on the phone, it was in the early evening, she said, Arthur, can you come over, I know this is very irregular, but we've been friends a long time, I'd appreciate it. I said, of course I would—I was, naturally, puzzled and curious, but I got in my car and I drove over to her house. She was sitting in her living room, quite agitated. There was a young man, blond-haired, with a ponytail sitting there too. Something was very wrong, I could sense it the minute I got there.

"Harriet said, I've had an accident, Arthur; I wonder if you could take a look at what's bothering me... I don't want to go to the emergency room; and I'm asking you to do this as a personal favor. She said, I'll pay you, of course. I said nonsense. Then we went into the next room, a sort of study, and closed the door; she was in some pain, I should add. She was badly bruised, but it was clear there was nothing major, no broken bones. Still, for a woman her age, over 80, you can't be too careful.

"I said, Harriet, what's this all about? And who's that young man? I don't like the looks of him.

"She said, 'That's Tommy. Never mind him.... I just want to know, do I need to get... well, medical attention?'

"I said: Harriet, tell me what happened.

"She said, An accident, Arthur. I fell down the steps.

"I said, Harriet, I've been around, I have experience with these things. That was no accident, and you never fell down the steps. I know those kinds of bruises. This is not a matter for me, it's a matter for the police. Now let me ask you again: who is that young man?

"She shook her head, and she said, again, that's Tommy. Forget about him. I said Harriet, really! You've got to call the police. This is... elder abuse. She came over to me and put her hand on mine. She said, Arthur, I can't do that. I can't go to the police. Trust me on this.

"You're afraid, I said to her; that's why you're so reluctant. And I said to her, that's only natural; the fear is natural. But you've got to take the first step, Harriet. Otherwise, these things will continue.

"She said, it's not the way it looks, Arthur. Believe me. Don't... don't even think about Tommy.

"I couldn't persuade her. I was tempted to go to the police myself, but she had been so insistent, so anxious to cover everything up. So in the end I didn't follow my inclinations.... I did what she told me to do. I wish now I hadn't."

Barbara said: "I told Dr. Swanson about my suspicions. I told her exactly what I told you. I'm more convinced than ever that she didn't die a natural death. Somebody killed her."

"Who signed the death certificate?" I asked.

"It wasn't Dr. Swanson," she said. "He was out of town, at a medical convention. It was Dr. Lober. He's at the clinic too. I'm not criticizing him: he didn't know Aunt Harriet. He just saw an old woman in her 80's who apparently had a heart attack and died peacefully in her sleep. Why should he think anything else?"

"And what do *you* think," I asked Dr. Swanson.

He said, "I don't know what to think. I was shocked when I heard about Harriet, that she was dead. But you know, I was busy with other patients, she *was* old, although I wouldn't have expected... she seemed in good health, very good health, for a woman her age. I just assumed it was a sudden attack: it happens. But now I'm not sure. I wonder about this... Tommy person. Barbara tells me they were actually married. I find that grotesque."

Barbara said, "I find it more than grotesque. I find it criminal. I never understood it. Never. He... must have had some kind of hold over her. Blackmail or something. We *know* she was paying blackmail."

"To Tommy?" I said. "What was he doing with the money? And all this business of bank accounts, phony corporate shells, and so on... does that sound like Tommy?"

She ignored this last remark: it was far too rational. She said, "Anyway, he *abused* her; that's absolutely clear."

The doctor said: "It's something I've seen before; you'd be surprised. Elder abuse, this sort of thing, I'm sorry to say it isn't rare. Sadly enough, it's often within the family. Or some younger person comes and gets attached to an elderly person, a man or a woman, the old person is lonely, weak.... And if they have money: well, you can guess what happens next."

Karen had been silent all this time, drinking her coffee. But suddenly she put down the cup, and burst out: "I can't believe you two are saying these things. I just can't believe it. Do you *know* Tommy? Barbara, how could you. You should know better, you really should. Tommy... OK, he's not a genius. But violent? Barbara, did you ever see the slightest indication, the slightest hint, that Tommy was violent?"

Barbara refused to get angry, that was clear. "Karen, I don't mean to criticize you. Please try to understand. We simply weren't around when the two of them were alone, were we? So how do we know...."

"I'm going to ask you again," Karen said. "Did you ever see *anything* to suggest what you're saying, that Tommy would lay a finger on Aunt Harriet? God, sometimes I think you've never met him. I'm asking you: *do* you know *anything*, anything at all, that points in that direction? Please, Barbara. Be honest."

"No," Barbara said, "I haven't got any proof that Tommy was, well, that way. But still, you have to admit: he must have had some kind of hold over her. He must have."

"And you think he *killed* her?" Karen said, incredulously.

"I don't know," Barbara said. "I honestly don't know. Look, suppose she was going to divorce him. He stood to lose millions of dollars. That's quite a motive."

Karen said, "This is ridiculous. Why should she divorce him? Did she ever say anything about a divorce?"

"No. But Aunt Harriet never said anything about *anything*. I mean, with respect to Tommy... why she married him, for instance. She never said a word to us. She went off with him, or he went off with her, to Las Vegas; at least that's what they said, and when they came back, she said, we're married. I just couldn't believe it. I tried to ask her, why she did such a thing, but she refused to say. Maybe she was scared. Karen, we just don't know."

Karen was sticking to her guns. She said, "All I can say is this: the whole idea is ridiculous."

"Is it ridiculous to think he beat her?"

Karen said: "Are we sure *anybody* beat her? Maybe she actually did fall down the stairs...."

"Oh sure," Barbara said, with heavy sarcasm. But Karen went on, "And if somebody did beat her, which I'm not at all sure about, how do we know it was Tommy?"

"Trust me: somebody did beat her," Dr. Swanson said. "Fortunately, it was just bruises, no broken bones, nothing that wouldn't mend quickly. But as to who did it, of course I don't know. But who else would it be? Who else was around?"

Karen just shook her head. She had no intention of conceding the point. The conversation began to take on a certain edge. Everybody had been quite civilized so far, but now I saw storm clouds gathering. "I'm not going to speculate, Karen," Barbara said. Her voice by now was barely polite. "I just want to stick to the facts. Frank, I want Arthur to make a formal statement. He's willing." The doctor nodded. "Can you draw it up, you know, so that it's all proper and legal?"

I said: "What do you mean, proper and legal?"

"You know. What do they call it, a deposition?"

I said, "that's really something else, a deposition, Barbara. Anyway, for what purpose are we taking down this statement?"

"For the record. The official record. I want to show it to the police. And I want my aunt's body exhumed or whatever you call that."

I wanted no part of this. "Barbara, these are serious criminal matters: I don't have that kind of practice. I really don't do that kind of work. I have no idea what it takes to exhume a body."

"Well," she said, I'm not giving up. Can you refer me to somebody?"

I said, "Really, Barbara...." But she was insistent. "Well, if you must... I do know a very good person."

"Please give me his name, then," she said, "I'm not taking this lying down."

It was time for Dr. Swanson to go. He said he had a patient, which I doubted, but he made his excuses and left. I was eager to leave myself, but Karen stopped me. "Can you stay for a while, Frank?" she said. "I want to talk about this some more. With you too, Barbara. I have something to say... and I want you to listen."

The atmosphere between the sisters was, well, fairly poisonous by now. With siblings, that's not too uncommon. I see it all the time in my practice. Then there's Celia's older sister. But we won't go into that.

"Well, out with it, Karen," Barbara asked, with ice in her voice. "I wish you'd be more cooperative!"

"Look," Karen said, "I'll tell you plainly what I think. In the first place, this idea that Tommy hit Aunt Harriet, or that he *killed* her—it's total nonsense. You can laugh at their relationship, or you can call it perverted, but they seemed to *like* each other. Tommy... he seemed to hang on her every word.... And Aunt Harriet, well, she was extremely fond of him. I know that for a fact."

"Oh, yes," Barbara said. "He hung on her every word. Yes. That's why he moved out, I supposed, and took up housekeeping with some tramp he picked up from a bar or a trailer camp or God knows where."

"Aunt Harriet never objected, did she?" Karen asked. I know it seems odd.... Anyway, listen to me. I have a very different idea. About Tommy. It just came to me. I think it explains pretty much everything, about their relationship. I think Tommy must be Aunt Harriet's grandson."

"You mean, it's Tommy, not Joe Pangea?" I asked.

"Please, Frank," Karen said. "Why can't there be *two* grandsons? Now that we know Aunt Harriet had a son, there could be dozens of grandsons. And granddaughters. And why not Tommy?"

Barbara said: "This is ridiculous. She married her own grandson?"

"Well... legally he wasn't her grandson, was he? If he was adopted, no more than this Joe Pangea; so.... Just listen to me for a while. When did Tommy appear on the scene?"

"Three years ago, maybe four," Barbara said. "Or five. I don't remember exactly."

"He came from nowhere," Karen said. "She never said anything to us, Frank. Suddenly he just appeared. He did yard work for her, odd jobs around the house; we thought she just hired him, a handyman, something like that. Then she gave him a room. From the start, she seemed to *like* him a lot. So, well, it started to look like... I don't know what it started to look like, but they were awfully thick. I asked her, Aunt Harriet, what's his last name? She said, we're going to call him Tommy Wingate. He doesn't have a last name. I said, Aunt Harriet, *everybody* has a last name. She said, well, not Tommy. He's been shunted from place to place. Now he lives here—that's what she said—so he might as well be Tommy Wingate. He's like a member of the family. She said that: those were her exact words. And that was that. Now at the time I thought, this is crazy. Now I'm not sure. If he was in fact her grandkid, what could be more natural than to give him your name?"

Barbara said, "I can't believe you're saying this, Karen. Is there a shred of evidence to back this up?"

"No. But we can check on it, can't we?"

"And this wedding—can you explain that, too?"

"It makes sense," Karen said. "He was her grandson, but not legally. We know now, from this young man, this Joe Pangea, that Aunt Harriet's son was adopted by some family. So his kids were not legally relatives of Aunt Harriet's at all—isn't that so, Frank?"

I said "I think so." I made a mental note to check it out in the California Probate Code. More homework I'd assigned myself.

Clients always assume you know these things by heart. Of course we don't.

"Well, whatever," Karen said. "Aunt Harriet must have thought so. So maybe she felt if she married him, he would inherit her estate, or part of it, which is what she wanted."

"Why not just make out a will, leaving him money?" I asked.

"Because... that's a good question, I know. I have an idea, though. Maybe she was afraid of *us*."

"Us?" Barbara asked. "Which us?"

"Us us. You and me, Barbara. She was afraid we'd contest the will if she left a pot of money to some young man who was hanging around her house. But if they were married, he'd have his rights. We couldn't do anything about it. So it... makes sense, doesn't it?"

I saw the point. "But," I said, "couldn't she accomplish the same thing by adopting him? Why not go that route? That seems more normal. Why go to Las Vegas and get married?"

"Who knows?" Karen said. "Maybe it just didn't occur to her. Maybe she thought you could only adopt kids, not adults."

Barbara had a deep frown on her face; and I could see that she found this whole topic distasteful. She said so in no uncertain terms. She had, as was obvious by now, very strong feelings about Tommy. He was a gigolo, a male gold-digger, or worse: he had taken advantage of an old lady. "He preyed on her," she said, "on somebody weak and lonely... and here he was, an attractive young guy.... It's one of the oldest stories on earth."

Karen was having none of this. "Weak? Lonely? Are we talking about the same person? Aunt Harriet was old, but she *wasn't* weak. Remember she was always the black sheep of the family. Mother never quite approved of her—she was always saying 'That Harriet' and talking about the disgrace to the family and so on. And Harriet had a will of iron. You *know* that, Barbara. When she made up her mind, well, that was that. You couldn't possibly talk her out of whatever it was."

"Tell me more," I said. "I only knew her when she was old. I never thought about her except as a feisty old lady."

"She was quite something when she was young," Karen said. "She loved to do outrageous things. I'm not the least bit surprised to find out that she had a child out of wedlock. Then when she married Joseph Wingate... he was twenty years older than she was, and the rumor was, she broke up his marriage. His first marriage, I mean. He was crazy about her. And rich, of course. But after she got married, well, then she was Mrs. Joseph Wingate, and people had to treat her with respect. I don't think she ever lost her zest for life, or her love for a kind of adventure. With older people, most of us can't ever see past the gray hair. We don't see there's a human being there, an actual human being. Somebody who was once young and vital, and maybe that somebody is still the same way, only *old* and vital. That was Aunt Harriet."

"So what? What's the relevance of this inspiring speech?" Barbara asked, and once more, I caught a heavily sarcastic, angry tone.

Karen ignored the nastiness. "Aunt Harriet was her own person. And she had a strong sense of right and wrong. Maybe she thought she owed Tommy something. You know, because he was her grandson. Maybe she thought, he's my own flesh and blood, but he never had the advantages he should have had."

"What advantages?"

"I don't know where Tommy came from, but obviously he had no education. He had been bounced around in foster homes. When he came here, he was just doing this and that around the house, raking the leaves, cleaning out the garage. He certainly didn't come from a privileged background. And if he really was her grandson...."

But Barbara was stubborn too: "Karen, I think he's nothing but a young thug. A good-for-nothing, lazy, stupid hoodlum. A punk who was capable of beating a helpless old woman: you heard what the doctor said."

The two sisters went on quarreling, and I felt more and more uncomfortable sitting there. I had nothing to contribute to the argument, and I decided it was definitely time for me to leave. Let them work it out for themselves.

"Hey kids," I said, breaking in, "I've really got to go." They hardly noticed me, and when I left, they were still bickering.

12

On the drive home I went over in my mind the things I had heard. On the basic question, about Tommy, I have to admit I was on Karen's side. I just couldn't picture Tommy beating up an old lady, least of all Harriet Wingate.

I couldn't picture him as a murderer either. It just didn't fit my image of him. Maybe minor shoplifting or smoking weed. Something like that, but never violence.

But other people apparently had less trouble thinking of Tommy as a violent thug. And I don't just mean Barbara. In a surprising development, I learned very soon that the police shared Barbara's opinion about Tommy Wingate.

In fact, they had even bigger and more shocking ideas. A couple of days after my meeting with Barbara and Karen, the police picked Tommy up, brought him to the police station, and questioned him for hours. The subject was an extremely serious charge. In fact, it was murder. But not of Harriet.

The victim was a man named Vincent Fosco. His dead body, badly decayed and gnawed on by animals, had been found buried in the foothills to the west of Palo Alto. He had been dead for some time. Weather, or predators, or erosion, or some natural or zoological source brought the body nearer to the surface. A hiker who had left the trail, to "answer the call of nature," saw something that looked suspicious. He went closer, recognized that he was looking at bones that could be human, and called the police.

A police investigation soon identified the body as Vincent Fosco, who indeed had been missing for over a year. The police also concluded that Fosco had been murdered. And the investigation also led inexorably, for reasons I did not know at first, to young Tommy Wingate.

I got my first inkling of this startling news from Tommy himself. I was sitting in my office, minding my own business (and the business of my clients), when I got a phone call from Tommy. I recognized his voice immediately.

"Mr. May..."

"Tommy, you can call me Frank."

"Uh... Frank... I guess... I mean...." I could almost smell agitation in his voice. He was quite upset about something.

I said: "Tommy? Is something wrong?"

He blurted it out: "Man, I'm in deep trouble.... I'm in deep shit—excuse me—and I got to get me some help."

"What kind of trouble, Tommy?"

"They're... trying to pin something on me. Man, it's really serious. They think I killed this guy."

"What guy?"

"Vince Fosco."

The name meant nothing to me. "Vince Fosco? I don't know the name. Should I? Who is he?"

"Some guy. A gangster. I mean, he's dead."

"And they think you killed him?"

"Christ, I don't know what they think. Maybe yes, they do. That's what they're hinting at. They... asked me all these questions. Man, I'm scared."

"You were in jail?"

"Naw... they let me go, but they said they'd need to talk to me some more.... I was there for hours, they asked me all kinds of questions... man, it was awful."

"Why do they think you killed this guy?"

"Shit, I don't know. They didn't tell me. They kept talking about evidence, evidence; I don't know what they mean. Mr. May, I think they're going to arrest me...."

It did sound serious. I said: "Tommy, you're right: you need a lawyer. Didn't they tell you that you didn't have to talk? You know, the Miranda warning?"

"Yeah, they said some sort of stuff.... And I didn't say any-thing, you know? I kept my mouth shut. They started asking all this stuff, and I said, I'm not saying anything. You know, without a lawyer? They said, OK, call a lawyer. But I don't know any lawyers. Except you, I mean. Then they let me go.... I don't know why. They said not to go anyplace, just stick around. Man, I'm scared."

"Tommy," I said, "Are you home?"

"Yeah, I'm home. But you gotta help me... you're a lawyer, right?"

"Right," I said. "But I can't really help you. I don't do crim-inal work. I can give you a reference, though...."

"Yeah, OK, sure. But... I got a problem, Mr. May. These guys cost money. Lots of money. And what I want to know is, do I have the money? I mean, can I get some of Harriet's money? I told you I didn't care about the money, and I was telling you the truth, honest to God, I'm not thinking about money, but things have changed, you know? I really need it now.."

I had to agree, Tommy did need money. Fighting a mur-der rap is not a do-it-yourself project. The man I had in mind, the one I was going to recommend, was Nolan Thom; Nolan is a friend of mine, and he's an excellent criminal lawyer. I'm not crazy about his clients, but criminal lawyers don't usually work with choir boys.

Nolan, I might add, was a large man, and his talents were also large. Raw talent costs a great deal of money.

I would have liked to ease Tommy's mind. I tried to. I told him I *thought* he could have the money; I was pretty sure he would get *something* out of the estate. But right now, I had to tell him, the estate was in a kind of tangle, it was a mess, what with all these wills and non-wills, and I couldn't be 100% sure of anything. I said I would get in touch with Nolan, and talk to him, and tell him exactly what the situation was.

"I'd really appreciate it, Mr. May. Man, I'm just sick, I feel like throwing up, just thinking about this...."

Accused of murder. That's not part of most people's daily routine. No wonder Tommy was upset. But I couldn't help wondering: how much of a surprise was this to Tommy? Had he no knowledge of this at all? No connection with this Fosco person?

"This guy Fosco, Tommy: did you know him? Why do they think you did this?"

"Man, how should I know? These cops...."

"Tommy, who *was* Fosco?"

"Hey, he was just some guy, Mr. May. A gangster, a crook, a really bad guy." That's all he seemed willing to say. Nothing more. Nothing to suggest why anybody would think that he, Tommy Wingate, had killed this particular crook. It seemed plain to me that he knew who Vincent Fosco was.

But Tommy admitted nothing.

I was wild with curiosity. There was so much I wanted to know. Life is full of surprises. Surprises add spice to life. Of course, there are good surprises and bad surprises. And then there are just plain surprises. Here I was, a lawyer, and for years I had dealt with Harriet Wingate. I drafted wills for her, I answered questions about estate planning. She seemed like a feisty but conventional old lady. Yet suddenly, I find myself enmeshed and engulfed in mysterious goings-on, suspicions that somebody murdered her, a gaggle of ridiculous wills, a weird and unnatural marriage, and now... Vincent Fosco. What on earth was this all about? Did Vincent Fosco have some connection to Harriet Wingate or her estate? Was it only Tommy he was connected with?

Much as I wanted to, I couldn't ask Tommy all the questions that were torturing me. He seemed extremely agitated, which was understandable. I knew he wouldn't answer my questions, even if I was bold enough to ask them. Still, what he *didn't* say, what he didn't volunteer, was significant. I didn't hear the usual phrases about being totally innocent, or that the whole thing was a frame-up, or ridiculous and that sort of thing. He didn't admit he had something to do with the death of Vincent Fosco, he certainly didn't confess anything, and yet, I wondered....

I let him go, called Nolan Thom, got through to him fairly expeditiously, explained what I could about the situation, called Tommy back, gave him Thom's number, and then went back to my work. Or tried to. Curiosity kept gnawing away at me. Predictably. How could it not?

Barbara came to my rescue, at least partially. She appeared at the office the next morning—without an appointment. As it turned out I was free, and I invited her to come in and sit down. She knew all about the situation, and was almost indecently eager to tell me what she knew. And I, of course, was almost indecently eager to hear.

"Do you know the latest?" she asked.

She was mildly disappointed to find out that I *did* know the latest: that Tommy was under suspicion and that this was in connection with the death of a man named Vincent Fosco. But it was clear that she had more information than I did.

"Barbara, tell me everything. I don't know the first thing about this business, except that Tommy called me, and was in a state of panic, and told me he was being questioned about this Fosco, who is extremely dead. By the way, I referred Tommy to a good criminal lawyer."

"I'm amazed you're helping him out," she said. "Why should you? He's rotten to the core, he's a psychopath! I've always suspected it and this... this proves it, once and for all."

"Well, I had to talk to Tommy," I said. "If I'm handling the estate, that is. He's a possible heir."

"Even if he killed Aunt Harriet?"

"No, of course not, not if he killed your aunt. In that case, he wouldn't get a dime. But Barbara, surely you don't think that Tommy...."

She said: "Surely I *do* think. If he could kill this Vincent Fosco, he could kill Aunt Harriet."

I said, "Well, okay: if he killed Aunt Harriet, he wouldn't inherit from her, no. That's plain. It's in the law. The Probate Code. But Barbara, we're a long way from that. There isn't any evidence. For all we know, she died a perfectly natural death. Anyway, would somebody please for God's sake tell me who this Vincent Fosco is?"

She said: "I don't know much about him. Karen knows a little more, she talked to Tommy, I think. I don't know why she's so fond of Tommy. Sometimes I think... well, never mind."

"You're not implying some sort of romance? Barbara!"

"Oh, I suppose not. But she always takes his side. And listen: if Tommy could marry a woman of 80, he could carry on with a woman who's only 53. Yes, I know: she's my sister. Anyway, Tommy has this... girlfriend, or whatever you call them nowadays. This live-in girlfriend. Sophie. So Karen is out of the picture, if she was ever in it."

"Barbara, could you please answer my question? About Vincent Fosco?"

"I told you I don't know very much. He was some kind of gangster or whatever. The police found his body in the woods, I guess you know that. Mostly a skeleton I think, chewed up by animals.... The body had been buried in a pretty remote spot, up in the hills, you know, toward the La Honda area. I don't know how they found it, whether somebody tipped them off, or somebody was digging or something—anyway, they found this body. It had no identification, but somehow they proved it was this guy, Vincent Fosco. Maybe through teeth. Don't they usually do it through teeth?"

"Teeth?"

"Isn't that how they identify bodies? With teeth? Honestly, Frank, I wouldn't know. Dental records. Or DNA, maybe it was DNA. You'd have to ask the police."

"But what does this have to do with Tommy?"

"I can't give you a definite answer," she said. "Not yet, anyway. Vincent Fosco, this man, the body they found—it was clearly murder. He was shot through the heart. I think they found the gun. All that Karen would tell me is that there was some evidence, something, whatever it was, that pointed to Tommy; there was some link between Fosco and Tommy."

"A link between Fosco and Tommy? What could it be?"

"Frank, I have no idea. I'm just telling you what I know. The police figured Fosco had been dead about a year. They can't be more specific than that. Karen thought they didn't have enough to actually *arrest* Tommy: they were hoping he would confess or say something incriminating. Anyway, they started investigating, oh, as soon as they found the body. That must have been the reason they came to Aunt Harriet's house the week before she died. You remember I told you about that."

"I do remember."

"She never breathed a word of it to me. I told you how puzzled I was. But now I understand. She was trying to protect Tommy, of course. Doesn't that make sense?"

"I guess it does."

"She was always trying to protect Tommy. God knows why," Barbara said.

"She... seemed to like him," I said timidly.

"More likely she was *afraid* of him," Barbara said.

I kept quiet.

Barbara went on: "I suppose they're still investigating the case, looking for something. I have no idea what Aunt Harriet told them. She was quite capable of lying to protect Tommy if she thought he was in trouble. But I don't know what happened. Really, I've told you everything."

"Do *you* know anything about this Fosco?"

"Absolutely nothing. I never heard his name before."

"And... Karen?"

"Also nothing. At least that's what she says."

"And you believe her?"

"I think I do. She was pretty positive," Barbara said.

"So what does all this mean, Barbara?"

"I don't know," she said. "Really. Still, I thought this was the right time to tell the police what *I* know about Tommy. About how he abused Aunt Harriet. And I did.'

"You didn't!"

"I most certainly did. And believe me, they were very interested. I gave them Dr. Swanson's name. You can be very sure they're going to check on this. And another thing: I told them what I thought about Aunt Harriet's death."

"You didn't!"

"Frank, you said that before. You're repeating yourself. Why shouldn't I? Why should I let Tommy—if it *is* Tommy—get away with murder?

"It's sheer guesswork, Barbara."

"I know it is. I admit it. But let *them* check on it. That's their job, isn't it? They'll exhume the body or whatever they do. Isn't that how they do it? In a way, I hate the idea. Poor Aunt Harriet. It's... disgusting; but I feel it's necessary. That way we'll know for sure what happened. And mark my words, you'll see that I'm right."

"Well... suppose you are, what good will that do, Barbara? I mean, exhuming the body. Your theory is, she was smothered, right? With a pillow. Does that leave, well, marks or bruises, or something? I have no idea."

"Nor do I. But maybe she was strangled. Oh, I admit, she didn't *look* strangled. Still, how would I know? Anyway, it's their business, Frank."

"I guess you're right," I said meekly. And that was the end of this particular conversation. To be honest, I did not expect much from the investigation. I turned out to be wrong.

13

All along I had been a doubter. From the very first. I thought Barbara was paranoid or worse. I thought her idea was completely preposterous. The idea that somebody murdered Aunt Harriet. You can be sure I'm telling this story with total honesty, because I am about to reach a point where I eat a very large portion of crow.

I won't beat around the bush. A few days later, Barbara called me again at my office. And she informed me, with a real air of triumph, that she had been right after all: Aunt Harriet had been murdered. It was now a proven fact.

"Barbara, how do they know? I mean, even though she's been dead more than a month, they can tell... that somebody smothered her with a pillow?"

"Forget the pillow, Frank. She was poisoned."

"Poisoned!"

"That's what I said: she was poisoned."

"But... the doctor's report, Barbara: the death certificate and all that...."

She said: "Doesn't mean anything, Frank. If you just thought, like that stupid Dr. Lober, that this was an old lady who died in her sleep, heart attack or something, well, you'd put that down on the death certificate. He never suspected a thing."

"And it was poison? Wow!"

"Yes, poison."

"What *kind* of poison, Barbara?"

"I don't know. They didn't tell me. And I'm not an expert on poisons."

I know even less about poisons. The only poison I know is ant poison. My kitchen is infested with ants. They are absolutely implacable. Nothing stops them. I spray and spray, and they always come back.

Could you use ant poison to murder somebody? Or rat poison? Fortunately, we don't have rats.

"Frank, are you there?"

I was there. But my head was reeling. "Do they know... who poisoned her?"

"Frank, how could they know? They just found out about the poison. Give them a little time."

"But *you* think it was Tommy?"

"Of course I do. I think he's violent. I *know* he's violent. And maybe he decided he was tired of waiting for poor old Harriet to die. She was taking her time about it. So he thought, I'll just hurry the process along. I wouldn't put it past him. Or that girlfriend of his either."

She seemed so sure of herself. I didn't feel like arguing with her; it would be pointless anyway. But I simply couldn't accept what she was saying. I couldn't match her words with the actual Tommy Wingate: dim, rather helpless, the guy with the ponytail and the scared blue eyes, sitting in my office, moving his knees nervously—I couldn't match this person with the other image: a brutal murderer, somebody who abused an old lady, beat her up, and then callously poisoned her.

And... poison? That seemed like an odd way to murder Aunt Harriet. Poison, I read somewhere, is a pretty rare way of killing people, despite all those Agatha Christie novels. It seemed particularly odd for Tommy. Why not smother Harriet Wingate with a pillow, if you wanted to get rid of her? That was Barbara's original thought. Or hit her on the head with a poker? Of course, poison, or the right kind of poison anyway, had its advantages. Nobody would think this was an unnatural death, if you did it cleverly. Still, the pillow would be just as good, I suppose, maybe better.

If it was poison, how did somebody get her to swallow it? Could it possibly be some sort of accident? I raised this issue with Barbara, and she said, "Absolutely not. Aunt Harriet wasn't taking any pills or anything of the sort—well, one little thing for cholesterol... no, it had to be someone doing it deliberately."

I mulled all of this over; and came to no conclusion of course. In a sense it was none of my business.

But then, I remembered, in a sense it *was*. I mean, if Tommy killed her, he wasn't entitled to inherit a penny from her estate; the laws of California were quite explicit on this point.

Money or no money, Tommy was in real trouble, that much was clear. It wasn't a great surprise, then, that Tommy called me again at the office. He sounded even more desperate than before. He had gone to see Nolan, he said. That part was OK. He said he liked him fine. "And he seemed smart. I guess he really knows his business." But now, he added, the police had this new idea, they were all over him with questions, about Harriet, something about poison....

"I know," I said.

"It's crazy, man; why would they think... it's nuts, it's just plain nuts, I couldn't do a thing like that."

I said: "I believe you, Tommy."

"Man, those cops... they can do things to you. It's scary what they do."

I babbled something in agreement.

Tommy went on, "She was my friend. I wouldn't hurt her. Man, I wouldn't hurt *anybody*. But especially Harriet.... Where do they get this stuff, the police?"

"I don't know," I said. "But... Tommy, if you're really innocent, and I think you are—well, just trust Nolan, he'll see you through."

He said, "Man, I hope so. I just got to get out of this.... And I really need that money. I just got to have the money. I need it so bad. They want to send me to the gas chamber, somebody's got to help me. I can't have one of those public defenders, they aren't worth shit. I heard that from somebody, I knew guys who got in trouble and they had those public defenders, it was like they had *nobody*, you know what I mean? This guy Nolan, he knows what he's doing, he's been around and stuff.... But he costs money, lots of money...."

I tried to change the subject; I wasn't sure what to tell him about money. "I know things look bad, Tommy," I said, "But don't get discouraged. Maybe it'll all blow over. You can maybe straighten things out. With an alibi, for instance. Were you home that night?"

"What night?"

"The night Harriet Wingate died."

He seemed confused. "The night she died? Yeah. Sure I was home."

"That's OK then. Can you prove it?"

"Prove it? I dunno... You can ask Sophie. That's my girl-friend. We were home... ate something, watched TV I guess. Went to bed. I mean, just an ordinary night, I didn't go out. She... she could tell them that, you know, tell them I was at home. Do you think they'd listen to her?"

Frankly, I didn't think so. I imagined the police would be extremely skeptical about an alibi provided by a live-in girl-friend. They wouldn't believe a word of it. I haven't had much experience with the police (fortunately). But my impression is they don't believe *anybody*. They have a jaundiced view of the human race. I suppose I would too, in their position. They're used to people lying and cheating and doing God knows what else. How much credence would they give to some bimbo who said, sure, Tommy, my boyfriend, was home the whole night?

But I didn't say want to say this to Tommy. Why get the poor guy even more upset? Instead I soothed him as best I could and told him to keep talking to Nolan. Nolan would have plenty of good advice. And as far as the money was concerned (I said), I'd look into it, and see what the possibilities were.

The problem of course was California Probate Code, Section 250. A person who "feloniously and intentionally kills the decedent" is not entitled to inherit. I suppose it was my duty to discuss that issue with Tommy. But right then I just didn't have the heart. And, unlike Barbara, I simply couldn't bring myself to think of Tommy as a killer.

14

Of course, my duties in this matter were, well, complicated. After all, Tommy wasn't my client. I'm not sure *who* I represented. Presumably the estate, although even that wasn't so clear, given the fact that wills seemed to appear and disappear magically in this affair. But assuming I did represent the estate, it was certainly relevant to know if Tommy was a murderer or was otherwise responsible for Harriet's death.

Still, to be honest, a large part of what motivated me was sheer curiosity rather than duty. The situation had the strangest elements. I couldn't make head or tail of it: a kid who married a woman who might just possibly be his own grandmother, another mysterious grandson who shows up out of the blue, the buried body of an Italian-American gangster nobody seemed to have heard of before, at least nobody in my circle of clients, a will leaving everything to nonexistent cats and, perhaps strangest of all, the news that somebody had actually poisoned Harriet Wingate.

I was intrigued. Can you blame me? Curiosity killed a cat, as the saying goes. In this case, it didn't kill me, and cats (as we know) had a role in this story, even though they seemed to be imaginary. But curiosity did lead me to do something a little bit questionable.

It was this: I got in touch with Sophie, Tommy's girl-friend. I went about it on the sly, one afternoon. Tommy, as I happened to know, had an appointment with Nolan Thom, so he was sure to be out of the house. This gave me a window of opportunity. I called his apartment and a woman answered, presumably Sophie. I hung up immediately; I just wanted to know if she was home. If I had any luck, she would stay there, too, at least long enough for my purposes. I got into my car, and drove as quickly as I could to Tommy's apartment.

Tommy and his girlfriend lived in Mountain View, which is just south of Palo Alto, and on the whole a lot less elegant and pricey. He lived in a section of town that was lined with cheap, low-rise, and quite hideous apartment complexes. You know the type: California is full of them. In Los Angeles alone there must be millions. They have a kind of pathetic stucco look. They are, of course, "modern," meaning they were thrown up in the last few decades. They have tropical plants growing around the perimeter, though the plants usually look a bit down at the heels. Occasionally, there's a sad little fountain somewhere in an interior courtyard, trickling a feeble stream of water.

Somebody who actually calls himself an architect designed these places, I suppose. Well, it certainly wasn't Frank Lloyd Wright or Le Corbusier. These "complexes" all look the same—as if they were stamped out with a cookie cutter. They give off a flavor of depressing monotony. At least the rent is cheap.

Cheap by California standards, that is. In Buffalo or Fargo, the rent would no doubt be considered outrageous.

Tommy's apartment was on the second floor in one wing of this dismal complex. I climbed the steps, noting that the metal railing was beginning to show signs of rust. I rang the bell and waited. Of course, Sophie could have gone out. But my luck continued to hold. I heard noises inside, and then she opened the door. She stared at me, and said, "Yes?"

She was striking looking, I'll give you that: very thin, almost cadaverous. She was, I'd say, in her late twenties. She was wearing a tie-dyed shirt, and a long print skirt. She was barefoot. Was it my imagination, or were her feet disgustingly dirty? That might be unfair. It's a thought that pops into my mind whenever I see somebody with bare feet. Her hair was extremely long, and she wore it tossed over one of her shoulders. It was jet black. She had sharp features—she wasn't unattractive, but her nose was a little bit too pointy for my tastes, and she had piercing eyes. She had an incredible jungle of vaguely Asian bangles and bracelets and necklaces around her neck and on her arms and wrists and at least five silvery but cheap-looking rings on her fingers. She was not smiling.

I said: "Are you Sophie?"

"I am. Who are you?"

"My name is Frank May. I'm a lawyer. I represent the estate of Harriet Wingate. I wonder if I could talk to you a bit."

Ah! Harriet Wingate was definitely the password. Open sesame. "Come in," she said.

The apartment was something of a mess. The furniture looked cheap—Salvation Army rejects, or something from Goodwill. I walked into a small living room. Sophie motioned me to sit down. Through a door I could also see a bedroom (the bed was unmade and rumpled), and a kitchen with dirty dishes in the sink. Neither Tommy nor Sophie was a finicky housekeeper, apparently. Somehow that didn't surprise me.

The sofa I sat on had seen better days. She said, "Can I get you coffee or something? Mineral water? A glass of wine? a beer?"

I said no. "You don't mind if I ask you some questions, do you? They might be, well, relevant."

"Relevant to what?"

"Relevant to... uh, the estate," I said. "I... represent the estate. The executor. This is about managing the estate." She gave me a quick glance. She was obviously shrewd enough to smell that there was something slightly off in my answer.

"What does that mean? Manage it how?"

Sophie was not going to be easy. I decided I had to be more honest than I had planned to be. "The question is, does Tommy inherit from the estate or doesn't he?"

"And what does that have to do with me, for God's sake?"

"Well, because... because Tommy is in trouble, as you probably know. If... if certain charges are borne out, well, he might not get the money he would otherwise get."

"So? Where do I come in? Does Tommy know you're here?"

"Not exactly."

"What do you mean, not exactly? Does he, or doesn't he?"

"Well, to be honest, he doesn't."

"So: this is behind Tommy's back, that's what you're telling me? Did you call on the phone before, and then hang up? You don't have to answer. It must have been you. What's this all about? You better explain what you're doing here. And spare me the bullshit."

"OK," I said. "I need to know some things, things you can tell me. About Tommy."

"About Tommy? Like what?"

"Like where he was the night Harriet Wingate died. He says he was here."

She drew a deep breath, and walked around the room. Then she gave a kind of weird little laugh. I could see I had hit on a sensitive point. Or had I? She said, "Mind if I make myself some coffee?"

"Go right ahead."

She disappeared into the kitchen, filled a cup with hot water from the tap, added some powdered instant coffee, and zapped it in the microwave for thirty seconds or so. I was glad I had turned down her offer. I have my standards when it comes to coffee. I don't need rare Colombian beans, but I draw the line at instant coffee.

She sat down with her coffee, emptied a packet of sugar substitute into the cup, twirled the spoon around, took a sip; and meanwhile played with the strands of her long, stringy hair. She was somewhat sexy, I have to admit, but I wondered how often she took a shower. This was pure prejudice on my part. Why did I imagine she was dirty? Because of her counter-cultural look? For all I knew, she was insanely fastidious in every regard. I know women like that.

"Is that a tough question?" I asked, trying to put myself forward a little more forcefully. "You didn't answer me. Was Tommy here that night, or wasn't he? It's a pretty simple question."

She laughed. But not a happy laugh. I said, "I guess you don't feel like talking."

She glared at me. "I do and I don't, OK? Go ahead and ask your damn questions, whatever you want. If I don't feel like answering, I just won't."

"I suppose this particular question, whether Tommy was home—is one of the questions you don't feel like answering?"

"Maybe. We'll get to that. Ask something else."

I took a pad of paper out of my briefcase, and pretended to take notes. This is a technique that cuts both ways. It makes some people nervous, but with other people, for some crazy reason, it loosens their tongues. In fact, I was just nervous, and needed to do something with my hands.

"What's your last name?" I asked.

"Is that important? Just call me Sophie."

I let that go for now. I wondered, though, why she didn't want to answer this simple and innocuous question. Maybe she was another one who called herself Wingate. Quite a popular name in this town. "Where and when did you meet Tommy?"

She said, "On the where: I'll take the fifth. On the when: I don't remember. It was, oh, say, a year ago. Maybe a little more."

"How long have you been... together?"

"Together. Oh you're something. You mean living together? Well, not long after we met, actually. I guess you can say we hit it off from the start. We moved in here about a year ago."

I was eager to know the exact date, but I didn't know how to ask. I was curious whether it was before or after Tommy drove to Las Vegas with Harriet Wingate, and had this May and December wedding. Then I had an idea:

I said: "Tommy made a trip to Las Vegas last year. Was it before or after that trip? I mean, when you moved into this apartment together?"

"After, since you're so curious. As a matter of fact, as soon as he came back, or very soon, maybe a week. It's my apartment; Tommy just moved in. Before, he was staying in Harriet Wingate's house. Well, you knew that. As to exactly when, well, I can't give you the hour, the minute, and the second."

"Who pays the rent around here? Do you work?"

"Yes, I work. From time to time. I was laid off recently. Since he moved in, Tommy's been paying the rent."

"With his own money?"

"I don't ask him where he gets it. We pay the rent on time. The landlord doesn't complain."

I put down my pen. "I have a feeling this next question, well, it's going to be one of those you won't answer...."

"Yeah? Try me."

"I'm just curious as to *why* you two got together. Frankly, Sophie, you don't seem his type."

"What's Tommy's type?"

"To be honest, dumb. He's a pretty dim bulb, don't you think? You don't seem that way. So what do you see in him?"

I thought she would be angry, but instead she found the whole thing amusing. "Well, he's good-looking, for one thing. Maybe he's a good lay, for all you know. But suppose I said, Tommy has a chance of becoming one very rich dude. Would that be enough of a reason?"

"I suppose."

"You suppose," she said with a sneer. "How come all these rich old geeks have trophy wives? You think it's their sex appeal, these fat old guys? Well, Tommy might get rich; and, what do you know, he's not old and fat, he's young and good-looking."

I almost admired her candor. "And you know what?" she went on, "I kind of like Tommy. Do you know him? You met him. He went to see you. You know, most people who know him, like him. That bitch Barbara doesn't. She's got it in for him. But other people, they like the guy. He's like a small puppy dog. That's how people think of him. A puppy dog."

"You too?"

"Not exactly," she said, and she came close to something resembling a smile. "I mean, I *live* with the guy. Anyway, you don't have sex with a puppy dog. I don't, anyway; there are people around who have sex with anything. Look: before we go any further, I want to get something straight. You say you're a lawyer?"

"I not only say it," I said, "I *am* a lawyer."

"A member of the bar, right? The California bar?"

Did she want to see a certificate? "Yes, I am. But... what are you asking for?"

"I want to know: is everything I say going to be confidential?"

"Well, maybe. Are you a client of mine?"

"Let's say I am. Let's say I might be. Let's say I might be in trouble...."

"What kind of trouble?"

"We'll come to that. Suppose I agreed to pay you for your time and for your advice: does that make me your client?"

"Sure." I said. This is the part where I wish I'd studied harder in my legal ethics class in law school, the part about conflicts of interest. I hadn't quite figured out how I could represent the estate and Sophie at the same time, if she had some secret that might affect the estate. "And then... whatever I say, it's confidential?"

"Absolutely." I vaguely recall some professor of mine telling me 'absolutely' was never the right answer. Probably it was the legal ethics teacher. But I guess that absolutely is never the right answer, in law or in life.

"OK: let's make that a deal. You're my lawyer. And we're talking here, and you're asking me, the night Harriet Wingate died, was Tommy home."

"Right. Was Tommy here at home or somewhere else? And were you with him."

She got up, went into the kitchen, and made herself another cup of her miserable coffee. Then she came back in, took a sip or two, and said, pointing to the cup, "You're sure you don't want some?"

I was sure. I repeated my question.

She sat down and looked away from me. She started stirring the coffee with a spoon, and took another swig. "Well," she said, "to be honest, the answer is yes and no."

"Yes and no? What does that mean?"

"As far as I know, Tommy never left our place that night. I think he was asleep in bed the whole night, right in his bed. I think he was in dreamland when... when Harriet Wingate died. But, I can't really prove it."

"Why not?"

"Because... *I* wasn't home. I can't give him an alibi, because I don't have one myself. But I can tell you this: I don't think he was at Harriet Wingate's house, if that's the thing you're getting at. I've heard all this crap, you know, she didn't die a natural death—I heard it was poison or something. And I heard, too, that they're trying to pin this thing on Tommy, which is completely ridiculous. First of all, it's ridiculous because he's Tommy. He wouldn't hurt a fly. Anyway, he wasn't there. He wasn't at Harriet Wingate's house."

"How do you know that?"

She gave a kind of raucous laugh. "I know that because... I was there myself."

"You were *there*?"

"Yes."

"At... Harriet Wingate's?"

"Yes."

This was something of a shocker, to say the least. No wonder she was interested in a lawyer. "You were at Harriet Wingate's?" I repeated.

"I said that once already, are you deaf?"

"You'd better tell me about it."

"OK, OK. I'll tell you the whole thing, from start to finish. I guess I better begin with something that happened the day before. The night before, actually. We were home, sitting right here. We had something to eat, I brought in some stuff from a Chinese restaurant, not that it matters, and Tommy was watching TV, some football thing. Then the doorbell rang. Big surprise. Nobody ever comes here. We opened the door, and it was Harriet Wingate."

"At your place?"

"Right. She came in, bold as brass—she was like that—and she said she had something to talk to Tommy about, something important, and would I get lost, or words to that effect. I said I'd go for a walk, and I left the room. I slammed the front door; but I didn't actually leave. There's a back entrance, and I went around and came back in. I stationed myself in the next room, the bedroom, with my ear pressed to the door. I wanted to hear what was so damn private and important."

"And what did you hear?"

"Plenty. I heard Harriet say she made out a new will, and she left her whole estate to charity. She said she left Tommy something, but she was vague about what it was exactly, and I figured it wasn't all that much."

"What did he say?"

"Oh, you know Tommy. He said, whatever she wanted, and she didn't owe him anything, and shit like that. Anyway: When she got done talking to Tommy, or when I thought she was done, I slipped out the back way again, went to the front, and slammed the door again, as if I just came in. They had no idea I was listening."

"You didn't like what you heard," I said.

"You bet! I didn't like it at all. I want to be rich—that's no crime, everybody wants to be rich. Tommy was my ticket to money, and now I could see it flying out the window. But I had an idea. From what she was saying, I figured she had the will in her house, so I made up my mind to go take a look at it, to see what it said."

"And... get rid of it?"

"I... well, I could have done that, yes. Why should I lie to you? I wouldn't have hesitated for a second. But that wasn't my plan, for a simple reason, because I didn't think I could get away with it. She, Harriet, might take a look or want to take a look, and if the damn thing was missing, she'd just do it all over again. I just wanted to see for myself—suppose she left him half a million; she was stinking rich, after all. Suppose what she meant was he would get half a million instead of three million, or something like that. Maybe it was still worth-while to stick with Tommy. And... another thing. What if she was bluffing? What if she was lying?"

"Why would she lie to Tommy?" I asked.

"I can think of some reasons. Because he might tell me about it, he'd say, Sophie, there isn't going to be any money. Maybe she wanted him to tell me that. She didn't want *him* thinking he was coming into a fortune."

"Why would she do that?"

"Well, different reasons. Maybe she would and maybe she wouldn't. Maybe she thought he'd get rid of me. She hated me, the old bitch. But I needed to know what the damn thing said. So... that's why I went to the house, the next night."

"But... she'd be there, wouldn't she? Mrs. Wingate?"

"No—at least I didn't think so. I thought the house would be empty. You see, Tommy called her up, Harriet, I mean, in the morning. I think he wanted to go see her about something: maybe the will, I don't know, maybe he was having second thoughts. Who knows. She told him she was going out of town —she was going to Carmel with Barbara that very day, and she wouldn't be back for two days. That's what Tommy told me. So I thought, the house is going to be empty tonight. This is my big chance.... I'm being honest with you, like I said. I knew it was risky, but I didn't care. I was willing to take a chance."

"When she was at your apartment, did Harriet Wingate say anything more about the will, or about *any* will? I mean, this case is full of wills."

"No... I told you everything. Well, almost. I think she said she left stuff to a bunch of cats, or something like that. Anyway, that's what she told Tommy. I thought to myself, I got to *know*. I'm not wasting my young life with this guy, if he's a loser, I mean, if there's no money. Look: I don't care how that sounds, like I'm some kind of cold-hearted bitch. Not that I give a damn what you think."

I mumbled something. She went on: "I told you, basically I like Tommy. Sort of. It hasn't been so bad, living with him. He's good-natured, in his own way. But I don't like him *that* much, enough to throw myself away on him, for life or for years and years. Anyway, let me go on.

"I didn't know then what I know now, that Harriet had told Tommy a big fat lie. She had no intention of going to Carmel or going *anywhere*. As far as I know. I think she just didn't want to see him, that's all. I don't know why. Anyway, I didn't know that she was lying, how could I? I thought she was going away, so she wouldn't be home. I thought I knew, too, where she kept the stuff. I wormed it out of Tommy once. He used to live there, you know, and he had a key. She had this desk, and there were papers in all the drawers.

"Anyway: I waited until evening. We had something to eat, pizza or something. Tommy was watching a football game on TV. I said to him, I've got to go out somewhere, I'll be gone a couple of hours, I'm taking the car. He said, where you going? Naturally, I couldn't tell him. I said it's something personal, some business with my family, I can't talk about it, you'll just have to trust me. Well, I could see he was bothered by that, I never talked about any family thing before, and maybe he was worried I was going to see some other guy. Tommy can get all insecure about that sort of thing."

"So what did you do?"

"Well... to be honest, I used a tried and true method. I started talking sweet to him, and then I came on to him pretty heavy; and we had sex then and there. When he was finished—it took all of five minutes—I told him how great he was, that sort of crap. Actually, he's nothing special, but guys always fall for that line, and I did the heavy panting routine, and after-wards I kidded him, boy you were fabulous; and I said, now, Tommy, if you're worried and suspicious, would I be going to some other dude after doing it with a great lover like you? He patted me on the behind. The TV had been going full blast the whole time, but it was half-time or the commercials were on or something, so then Tommy went back to watching his game, meek as a lamb. I put my clothes on, and I went.

"I had a copy of the key to Harriet Wingate's house. I took Tommy's key one day when he wasn't looking, and I went to Home Depot and had a copy made. I thought it would be a good idea to have a key to that house, don't press me on why. Anyway, it *was* a good idea. I got in the car and drove off. I parked a couple of blocks away from Harriet's house, and I walked quietly up to the house; there was a car parked in front, I didn't think anything of it at the time, but now it seems important.... There was also a light on, but I didn't think anything of that. People always leave lights on when they go away.

"I fit my key into the door, and I went inside. I don't know if you've been there, but there's a living room and a kitchen and dining room downstairs, and upstairs there's two bed-rooms and a kind of study. I went up to the study. That's where I wanted to look for the will. I tiptoed into that room... and then I heard a noise. I tell you, I was scared to death. I mean, I freaked out; the place was supposed to be empty. Now I heard something upstairs. Noises... voices...."

"Did you see who it was?"

"Not then, but later—well, not really, I never saw any-body, but I did get a glimpse, I'll come to that. At that time, I only heard the voices."

"How many voices?"

"I don't know. Maybe two. Maybe a man and a woman, but I can't be sure. Anyway, as I said, it freaked me out totally. I had turned on a light, and now I turned it off. I decided to get out of there as fast as I could. But then I heard the sound of somebody, coming out of Harriet's room, and heading down the stairs. I ducked down behind a sofa, in the study, so that nobody could see me. Then I listened, until the person opened the door and went out...."

"Did you see who it was?"

"Not really. Just a passing impression. I didn't see the face at all... just a figure. Look, I was breathing so hard, my heart was in my mouth. I didn't know who this was, a burglar or what. Later on I realized Harriet had been in the house, so maybe it was her voice I heard, or maybe it wasn't, but at the time, I thought I was alone in the house with some guy, maybe a criminal, and I was scared."

"You don't have *any* idea who it was?"

"Not a clue. I told you, I didn't see the guy's face."

"How do you know it was a man?"

"I saw the clothes, out of the corner of my eye, men's clothes... maybe blue jeans, I don't know."

"Women wear blue jeans."

"I know... look, I can't be sure about anything. I *think* it was a man. And I think it was a young man, Tommy's age or even younger, but I can't tell you why, maybe it was the way he bounded down the stairs."

"And you're sure it wasn't Tommy?"

"It wasn't Tommy. Besides, he was home. I told you that."

"OK, OK. Did you tell all this to the police?"

"Are you kidding? Of course not. Nobody saw me. Was I going to admit I broke into that house? Was I going to tell Tommy I was sneaking around, and had a copy of his key made, and all the rest of that? I'd be crazy to do that. I'm just telling you, and it's confidential."

"But... that person," I said, "maybe he was the one who gave her the poison."

"Look," she said. "I don't want to be involved. I don't give a crap who gave her poison, or anything. She's dead: that's all that matters. Count me out."

"All right. I hear you. So... then you just went home?"

"I waited a few minutes. Till I was sure the guy was gone. I thought I heard the sound of a car. The house was all quiet, but of course, I didn't know if there was anybody there or not. I practically crawled to the front door, then I opened it as quietly as I could, and went outside. The car, the one I saw before, well, now it was gone."

"Obviously you didn't catch the license number."

"Obviously."

"What kind of a car was it?"

"I don't know. Small car. I think it was a Honda Civic. I used to have one of those, an old beat-up Civic."

"What color."

"I don't know. It was dark outside, remember? Anyway, I hid in the bushes for another five minutes, then I went and got in my own car. Then I drove home. When I got there, Tommy was in bed, fast asleep, snoring away. I was nervous and upset, and disappointed too, because I never found the will, I mean. I decided to look around our place.... Tommy is a very heavy sleeper, I wasn't worried he'd wake up and see me.

"Tommy has a desk, not that he uses it much, but he puts his mail on top, and bank statements, and so on, and a bunch of stuff in the drawers. He's very sloppy about those things. I pay most of the bills, he gives me money. Anyway, I found this envelope from Harriet, sitting in a drawer. Sealed envelope. I steamed it open, and I saw that it was a will, a handwritten will. It left half of the money to Tommy and the rest to that bitch and her sister. That's more like it, I said to myself. But then I got worried: suppose this other will is somewhere, this stupid will, the one she talked about, the one about the cats or whatever. Suppose it's more recent. It's got to be more recent.

If so, then this one, the one in the envelope, wouldn't be worth a thing. I didn't know what to do...."

"Let me guess. You ripped off the top of the will, the part with the date; and then you sealed up the envelope again."

"Exactly. That gave us at least a fighting chance, I thought: we could argue that this will might have been the last one.... So... anyway. Well, you can see why I don't want to tell these stories to the police, I'd be in deep shit, wouldn't I? Tampering with a will, breaking into a house. But I'll tell you, frankly I don't like the idea of pinning a murder rap on Tommy."

"And Tommy doesn't know about this business with the will? He doesn't know that you tore up part of the will?"

"You think I'm crazy? Naturally, I didn't tell him. Don't you go telling him either. I told you these things in confidence. I said you could be my lawyer; I'd pay you."

"Great," I said. "And where would you get the money?" I didn't really care about the money. I was just reacting; she irritated me, for obvious reasons. Confidentiality, of course, doesn't depend on an exchange of money. That much seemed clear.

"What do you think? I'd ask Tommy. Sure, the gravy train has been temporarily derailed, since Harriet Wingate isn't around anymore to pay the bills, but if Tommy comes into that money...."

I said, "If. It's a big *if*, Sophie. You prove he had nothing to do with killing Harriet Wingate, the money is as good as his. If not, well, I don't know."

"What do you mean?"

"If he killed her, he doesn't get a cent."

She put down the coffee cup. "I tell you, Tommy never killed anybody. That guy who ran down the stairs... Maybe *he* killed her. But I can't identify him, I couldn't pick him out of a lineup. I told you, I don't even know for sure that it was a man. I just *think* it was."

"If we could find that guy...."

"Fat chance," she said.

We had both run out of things to say. She brought her coffee cup into the kitchen, and added it to a heap of dirty dishes in the sink. Then she came back, and ostentatiously looked at her watch. She said: "Maybe it's time for you to go. Tommy should be back any minute."

Tommy's prompt return was actually pretty unlikely, but I was perfectly happy to take the hint. I left, frankly somewhat confused and somewhat harassed, unsure what to do next. I didn't know if she was telling me the truth. I did believe a good deal of it. She had actually been inside Harriet's house. That was what we lawyers call an admission against interest, and she wouldn't lie about that. But did the story clear anything up? Or did it just add to the mysteries that surrounded this case? At least she explained why the holograph had the date torn off and who did it.

I didn't go directly home. Instead I drove around a bit, trying to think. Nothing came to mind. I parked the car and thought even harder.

She said she saw a man who came out of Harriet's bedroom and headed down the stairs. A young man, she thought, but she couldn't be sure. Who could this be? And what was this person doing in Harriet's room? Was she dead or alive at the time? Did this person *kill* her? If so, how? By forcing poison down her throat? That seemed so unlikely. And if he did this, why?

So many questions; and so few answers.

And yet....

I didn't know it then, but I was on the verge of finding out the answer to at least some of the puzzles. Less than a week later, I came to know who Sophie saw in the house, and why that person was there.

But before that happened, I took a number of necessary steps with regard to the Estate of Harriet Wingate. In the first place, I filed the torn holograph with the Probate Court, and I set the process in motion that would end (I hoped) with admission of the will to probate. I wanted the court to approve this will, despite the missing date. I wanted to have Barbara named as executor, and I filed a petition with the Court to have her named to that position. I was going on the assumption that the torn holograph was the real will, the last will, the only will that counted. Of course, I said to myself, who knows how many wills are going to appear mysteriously? There's been a positive epidemic of wills. But so far only one of these will was actually in our hands: the torn holograph. And so that was the will which I filed.

In the event, no more wills did show up. Did that mean the holograph was the winner, in the end? That it ultimately decided who got what? Wait and see.

One thing though: by now I was reasonably sure we had heard the last of the infamous cat will. I wasn't sure *why* Harriet had ever executed this crazy will, which so obviously was not meant to be her last will and testament. I did have an idea what the point of it was, and I will share this idea with you in more detail later on. The way I figured it, this will was some kind of red herring. She had it drawn up for the purpose of sending a message, and when the message was sent, she destroyed the will.

But who was supposed to eat the red herring (if that's the right idiom)? That was the question. Tommy was one obvious answer. According to Sophie, Harriet dropped in on the flat she shared with Tommy, she chased Sophie out of the house to have a heart-to-heart talk with Tommy, and proceeded to tell Tommy she was cutting him out of her will. Apparently she told him about the cat will. At least that was Sophie's account.

Did this make any sense? At one level it did. Sophie seemed to know about the cat will, and this lent credence to her story. She said she listened in on the conversation; so that part made sense. At another level, the story made no sense at all. For one thing, Tommy had lived in Harriet Wingate's house, Tommy knew Harriet very well. He was certainly aware that she had no cats, that she hated cats, that she was allergic to cats, and so on. Then why tell him about a will which was so patently ridiculous?

Is it possible that Harriet, who was nobody's fool, *knew* that Sophie was listening in? That this was a charade for Sophie's benefit? Maybe she winked at Tommy when she told him about the cat will. Maybe she wanted Sophie to think the gravy train wasn't stopping at this particular station anymore. It wouldn't be strange if she mistrusted Sophie. She might have thought that Sophie was a gold-digger, or that in any event she was the wrong partner for Tommy.

The wrong partner for Tommy? For her *husband*?

God, that sounds strange! But this was a case where the usual rules didn't seem to apply. After all, the grieving widower came to his wife's funeral with his current girlfriend! In this sort of context, doesn't *everything* sound strange?

15

For various reasons, I felt I needed to check things with Tommy himself. I wanted, for example, his version of the conversation with Harriet, assuming he would give it to me. I tried to get him on the telephone. I was hoping he'd be there at home, but without Sophie... and I was in luck. Tommy was there, and answered the phone—I guess it wasn't a good day for job-hunting—and Sophie was apparently out. I asked him if he was alone. He must have thought it was an odd question, which it was. He said, sure he was alone, Sophie was out some place. Well, could you come see me, I said. And... could I ask you not to mention this to your girlfriend? This is private stuff, I said. He said OK, and made no other comment.

Tommy was a no-comment kind of guy.

He came to see me pretty promptly. He was, after all, distinctly underemployed: what else did he have to do? The last time he had talked to me, he said he was looking for a job. I wondered how hard he was looking.

"Good to see you, Tommy," I said.

He sat there fidgeting. I was struck again by those vacant blue eyes. He had a fresh rubber band around his ponytail. He was wearing a jeans jacket over a white T-shirt. At least he looked clean.

He seemed extremely nervous. As if he was wondering what this was all about. He had the look of a scared rabbit. Or—what's the expression?—a deer caught in the headlights. I don't think he was comfortable sitting in a lawyer's office.

Even with me, and I'm the least intimidating man I know. That's my self-image at least.

I said: "I wanted to bring you up to date. I mean, you're one of the heirs."

"Oh, sure. Yeah, heirs," he said.

"I filed the will," I said. "You know, the short one, the one in the envelope, the torn one. The one you gave me. That's the only one I've got at the moment, so we're going to assume it's all valid, and it leaves half the estate to you, Tommy. As you know."

He nodded and continued fidgeting.

I went right to a question that intrigued me, even though it had really nothing to do with the issues. "I have to ask you some questions, Tommy. You don't mind, do you? It's necessary, for the estate...."

"Sure."

"You call yourself Tommy Wingate, right? But that isn't your real name, is it?"

"It *is* my name. Anyway, it is now."

"But... not the name on your birth certificate."

He said, "I never saw no birth certificate."

That was fair enough. I never saw mine either. Still, I pressed on: "I mean, Tommy, what did you call yourself *before* you called yourself Tommy Wingate?"

I should have known I would get a totally evasive answer. He said: "I had all kinds of names. I had these foster parents, they had all different names."

"And... your father's name?"

"He's dead," he said, as if that was an answer. He looked more and more uncomfortable. I dropped the subject of names.

"When did he die, your father?"

"Man, I don't know. I never saw him. I don't even know his right name...."

"But you're sure he's dead."

"I guess he's dead. My mom said he was dead."

"And your mother?"

"She's dead too."

"But you knew her...."

He was looking even more uncomfortable, if that was possible. I felt guilty. These questions were completely irrelevant to our legal business, and I wondered if he was beginning to catch on to that fact. I said, "I'm sorry. You don't have to answer these questions... about your mother, if you don't want to."

"I guess I don't."

I switched the subject. "There's one... uh, detail I want to clear up," I said. "I understand Mrs. Wingate came to see you, the night before she died. At your apartment."

"Uh, what night was that?" he said, blankly.

I gave him the date, and he started fidgeting even more in his chair. "I'm not good on dates and stuff," he said, "I dunno. I don't really remember... She did come over sometimes...."

This was an obvious lie. I just couldn't let it go by. "Come on, Tommy," I said. "This is really, really important. Try to remember. The night before she died. You were in your apartment. She came to see you."

"She came to see me? Who told you that?"

I felt trapped. I couldn't mention Sophie's name. I punted: "Never mind how I got that information, Tommy. You know, we have our sources. Don't forget, the police have been investigating you. They have ways of finding these things out."

He had a look of sheer panic. Had I overdone it? I got up, went over to him, and put my hand on his shoulder. "Tommy," I said. "Just remember: I'm on your side. I'm your lawyer. Everything you say to me is said in confidence. I can't tell anybody anything you say, it's just between you and me."

He seemed relieved. I went on: "Now, I *know* she came to see you. You've got to tell me about it. It's really important to, uh, help you out—you know, get you the money, the money for Nolan and all that. But you've got to cooperate with me, you've got to trust me, you've got to tell me the truth. You can lie to anybody else, but you mustn't lie to me."

That seemed to work. After all, he did need the money, and badly. He saw me as the key to the money box, so to speak. He said, "Yeah, she came. Harriet. She called me first, and said she wanted to talk to me. I said, sure thing, I'll come by. She said, that's alright, I've got things to do in town, I'll come to your place. She liked to do things her way; she had a car, she drove it everyplace. Anyway, she came by...."

"To your place?"

"Yeah."

"What time was that?"

"I don't remember."

"Was it six o'clock, or seven o'clock or midnight or what?"

"Maybe seven o'clock. I told you, I don't remember."

"Was anybody else there?"

"Well, my girlfriend. Sophie. She was there."

"So... she's a witness? To what Harriet Wingate told you?" Pretty sly, I thought.

Tommy took it all wrong. "Jesus, what a mess I'm in.... You need a witness? But Sophie... she wasn't there... I mean, she was there, but she didn't stay. Harriet wanted to talk, uh, private with me. So she asked Sophie, you know, politely... could she leave us alone; and Sophie went out, went for a walk I think. Jesus, I wish I had known..."

I said: "It's OK, Tommy. We don't really need a witness. Just tell me straight what happened. I think I can guess: she came to talk to you about her will."

"Her will? What will?"

"A will... the one we talked about once before. A will that left a bunch of money to take care of cats."

"Man, are you crazy? Why would she talk about that? She never... I told you, cats made her sick. She used to break out, she'd get a rash, you know? Even if the cat wasn't around, I mean, just someplace near, she had this allergy thing...."

"But she *did* make out that kind of a will: we know it. And she came to talk to you about it."

"No such thing. No way. I don't know what you're talking about," he said.

"She didn't talk about her will?"

"I told you: no, she didn't."

"Then what *did* she talk to you about?"

"Different things."

"What does that mean, Tommy? What kind of things?"

"Personal stuff."

"Tommy, you've got to tell me: what do you mean, *personal stuff*? What did she talk about?"

"She... OK. I'll tell you. She wanted to talk about Sophie. She said, she didn't like her, she didn't like Sophie. I mean, she thought Sophie wasn't right for me. She said she just wanted the money, she said Sophie smelled money, Harriet's money; she said she was no good, and... stuff like that."

"So, you had an argument?"

"An argument? With Harriet? No way."

"You just listened to what she said, and you just took it in and said nothing? She was telling you to break up with your girlfriend, and you just sat there like a bump on a log? I can't believe that, Tommy."

"I'm telling you the truth, the honest-to-God truth, like I said I would. We talked: we talked it over. But we didn't argue about it, no! I mean, we never argued about things. I never argued with Harriet. Never. We just talked."

"And what did you decide?"

"Nothing."

"What do you mean, nothing?"

"I mean: nothing. We just talked."

I was getting exasperated. Tommy's passive resistance was really tiresome. I had to drag every word out of him. Of course, if he was telling the truth, and if Sophie had been listening in to the conversation, then maybe she had a genuine motive for killing Harriet Wingate. Harriet Wingate was her enemy. Harriet Wingate wanted to take away her meal ticket. And, by Sophie's own admission, she had been at the house that very night....

If Tommy was telling the truth. *Somebody* was lying here. Sophie told this elaborate story, that she overheard a conversation about the cat will, and Tommy categorically denied it. One of them was lying. I voted for Sophie. To me, Tommy was not smart enough to dream up an elaborate network of lies. There I was probably wrong. You don't have to be a rocket scientist to tell lies.

But why would Sophie make up such a story? And if she was lying, how come she knew about the cat will? Who told her about it? Who else knew about the cat will?

I couldn't answer these questions, so I went back to the tough job of trying to get something out of Tommy. "OK," I said. "You just talked. But I guess Mrs. Wingate never did convince you... the two of you are still together, you and Sophie."

"I guess we are," he said.

"Maybe you didn't really believe the things Mrs. Wingate was telling you. About Sophie. Why was she so against your girl friend?"

"I dunno. The money I guess. Nothing else," he said.

Was this another lie? Maybe. But what could I do? I tried something else: "Could it be that... she was jealous?"

He stared at me, with a look of total befuddlement. "What's that, Mr. May? Jealous? I don't get you."

"Jealous. Just plain jealous. Is that so hard to understand? After all, the two of you were *married*."

Somehow he seemed surprised by that remark. "Yeah, OK, right: we were married. But... man, you just don't understand."

"What don't I understand?"

"About me... and Harriet. You don't understand. She... was my friend, you know? I trusted her."

Again, he had a scared look on his face. I could see this had been a painful session for Tommy, and I was worried that I might have lost his confidence. I wanted to avoid that, at all costs.

But this meant backing away from some of my plans. I had wanted to ask him about Vincent Fosco: who was he, what was his connection with Tommy, and all that; but I could see this wasn't the time or the place. So I switched back to more mundane business. I explained to Tommy again as gently as I could that he stood to get a lot of money, but that he would lose it all in the "very unlikely event" (and I added that Nolan is going to make sure it's "not only unlikely, it's just plain impossible") that he was convicted of killing Mrs. Wingate. "And remember that I'm on your side, too, Tommy," I said. Which was something of a lie, since "my side" was technically the estate, and if Tommy really did kill Harriet Wingate, I was most definitely *not* on his side. In fact, my duty would be to resist his claims with all my lawyerly guile and strength. But a little white lie, I thought, was definitely useful here.

We talked a little bit about the money, how much it was, and for the first time, Tommy seemed to show some interest in these financial affairs. He asked when he could get hold of some of this money. Of course he said he needed the money, to pay his lawyer: "these guys don't work for nothing, you know? I just can't believe how much money he wants." But he had other things in mind, too, he said. He became talkative, actually, for the first time in my presence. "I want to go to school, vocational school," he said. "I think I could fix computers or do something like that. They make a lot of money, the guys who fix computers. Harriet had a computer and one of those laser printers, she didn't use it much. But anyway, the computer was always doing weird things, she had to call somebody. Those guys really charge. I thought, boy, now there's a job. And I want to get a sports car. I always wanted one. And maybe a motorcycle. I was going to get one, before.... Well, Harriet said it was OK. She said, Tommy, you really want a motorcycle? And I said, sure, I'd love to ride one of those suckers, you know, vrooom... vroom.... She laughed, and she said to me: Tommy, if you get a motorcycle, would you take me riding on it? I said, sure, no sweat. You'll be the first one I'll take. And she liked that, you know? She said, I always wanted to ride on one of those things. Jesus, I wish I had gotten one. I wish I had taken her for a ride. She would have really loved it."

He seemed genuinely moved. I tried to imagine the two of them, Tommy in a leather jacket and Harriet in a motorcycle helmet, sitting in front of him, riding off with a roar into the sunset. I simply couldn't picture it. I guess there was more to Harriet Wingate than I had ever been aware of.

People absolutely baffle me. Not just Harriet. People in general. They really do.

16

Time has a way of zipping by. It rushes past you, and it's all a blur, like a streaker rushing by you on the stage and into the wings before you're even aware. I don't know where time goes, but it goes. Anyway, I was extremely busy in the office those days, which is a good thing, because that's where my money comes from. I had very little time to spend on the Wingate estate, but I didn't neglect it entirely.

There were a number of aspects of the estate that troubled me as a lawyer. I now knew why Tommy's holograph was torn and who tore it. But I didn't really know the date on the holograph. I had forgotten to ask Sophie whether she had kept the scrap of paper she tore off. When I got around to asking her, she said she hadn't; and when I asked what the date *had* been, she claimed she didn't remember. She might be telling me a lie, but even so, how would I know?

Then there was the will that Harriet discussed with Joe Pangea. We had a copy of that will, and it was almost certainly *later* than the cat will and the holograph. It was probably the latest one of all.

Of course, that will was also among the missing. But had Harriet Wingate destroyed it? I was sure she had gotten rid of the cat will, but why would she get rid of this later will? If I had to guess, I would guess that she *didn't* get rid of it; that somebody lifted it. Maybe the same somebody took the opportunity to kill her. Killed her by forcing poison down her throat —if that's what he did. Or she did. A really strange way to kill somebody, I thought. But then, what do I know about ways of killing people? It's not my line of work.

Maybe the poison wasn't forced down her throat. Maybe somebody gave her a cup of tea laced with poison. Or put it in some medicine. That's the way they do it in a lot of mystery stories. You put the poison in hot milk, or a cocktail, or a tonic, whatever that is, or some other liquid, or the old person's medicine. Later, you could wash the cup or whatever you put the poison in, and then who's to know?

Suppose we could show that somebody else took that will: what then? Ah: then it would be possible to offer the copy as her real will. Of course, a copy isn't a will, but if the will has been destroyed illegally, you can show the court the copy as evidence of what was in the real, legitimate will. That was crystal clear, under California law. The Pangea will (that's what I called it) was pretty much the same in its essentials as the will I drew up, and even the holograph had the same three basic beneficiaries—Tommy, Barbara, and Karen. The main difference, of course, was $75,000 to young Joe Pangea.

I felt I had a duty to keep him informed of this possibility. I checked in with Barbara before I spoke to him. She was not too keen about this. "It's not the money," she said, "but who is he? He's come out of the blue, and now he wants $75,000."

"That's a bit unfair, Barbara," I said. "Your aunt wanted him to have the money. He's a blood relation. It's not like he demanded it or anything. As it is, his chances of collecting the money are pretty remote. I just think I ought to speak to him, tell him what the situation is."

She agreed, somewhat reluctantly, and I left a message for Joe Pangea on his answering machine. He called me back the next day. I asked him whether he could come see me, and he said he could.

"Are you sure?" I asked him. "I know it's hard to get down here on public transportation."

"I've got wheels," he said. "An old car, it's as old as the hills. But it runs. And I've got some friends at Stanford. I don't mind at all." We set a date and in fact agreed to have lunch together—that was best for me, it turned out, because I had a pretty heavy day otherwise, wall-to-wall clients. It turned out to be an important lunch, not that the lunch itself was anything special. We went to a local Chinese restaurant, frankly mediocre, and I ate too much, which I often do. The restaurant, despite denials, was heavy on the MSG. I gobbled down my sweet and sour pork, and then went into my spiel, despite a headache. Joe listened carefully to what I had to say, nodded his head, and said very little. He looked very Joe College, with his short hair and his Cal sweatshirt.

"Sure, I'd like the money," he said, "but I understand what you're saying, I understand it's a long shot."

"You could fight for it," I said. "I told you about how, in California, it's possible to probate a lost or destroyed will. Possible but difficult. I'm attorney for the estate, so it's my duty to carry out the will of Harriet Wingate. I mean will in both senses: since all we've got for a legal will is that torn holograph, at the moment, well then that's what I've got to take as my Bible. I suppose there's a chance your will might turn up. If it does, then my duty would be to carry out that one."

"You do what you have to," he said. "I'm not going to make a fuss. Whatever happens, it'll happen."

He seemed quiet, almost subdued. I had the impression, as he played aimlessly with his chopsticks, that he had something on his mind, something that he wanted to tell me. "A penny for your thoughts, Joe," I said. But he just smiled and said nothing.

We finished, I paid, put the receipt in my pocket—this was, after all, an expense of the Harriet Wingate estate which, of course, the estate could well afford—and we got up to go. "Where are you parked?" I asked.

"Just down the street here. I was lucky. I found something right nearby. Parking is usually a bitch."

"I'll walk you to your car," I said.

We walked and chatted. I asked him about his classes, his exams, his future plans. "Not sure," he said. "Hey, maybe I'll go to law school." I said, "Why not? Everybody's doing it." We walked for a block or two. "Here it is," he said. He pointed to a rickety old Honda Civic, and something clicked in my brain. I grabbed his arm, pretty vigorously. I guess I was more excited than I realized. "Joe," I said. "We've got to talk."

He seemed startled, as well he should have been. After all, we *had* been talking, and my tone of voice would have startled anybody. "What about? Didn't we talk already?"

"Something important," I said. It was the car. It rang a bell. Sophie, who couldn't have been lying about *everything*, said she saw an old car, a Honda Civic, parked in front of Harriet's house. She thought there was a man in the house, and she thought he had driven off in the Civic. A young man, she said. Of course, she could have been mistaken. And there are lots of old Civics floating around. This is California, after all. Nobody buys an American car around here: that would be considered downright gauche. So it could have been a coincidence. And yet....

"I... I could stay a while, I guess," he said, more or less stammering. "What's the matter?"

"Joe," I said. "I think you've been lying to me."

"Me? Lying?"

"You never saw Harriet Wingate? Never actually met your grandmother? Never?"

An old man, walking by, stared at me. I guess my voice was pretty loud. There was a bench nearby, on the corner. I motioned Joe to sit down. On the corner of the bench, a young woman sat, her eyes closed, face toward the sun. When we sat down, she got up and went away. People like to be alone sometimes. "Joe, answer my question."

He looked nervous now. "What are you getting at, Mr. May? Why are you asking these questions?"

I said: "Joe. Your car. Somebody saw it."

"What do you mean? Saw it where?"

"Be honest with me, Joe. Don't fool around. Your car was parked outside Harriet's house. The night she died. And you were in the house. You were upstairs. You went down the stairs, you came out the door and drove off. In that car."

Joe was nobody's fool. He said: "Who told you that? I don't believe it."

"Never mind who told me. What is it you don't believe?"

"I... I don't believe your whole story. There are lots of cars like this... Two of my buddies at school have Civics."

"Not with this particular number on the license plate," I said.

I was bluffing, of course, but I scored a direct hit. I could see it on his face. But he still tried to wriggle his way out. "No way," he said. "I don't believe you. Why would somebody copy down the license number just because they saw a parked car outside somebody's house?"

"Come on, Joe," I said, as brazenly as I could. "They had reasons. A woman died in that house later on." Then I added, in a more gentle voice, "Look, Joe. I'm the lawyer for the estate. You can tell me anything you want, in confidence. You were there. You might be the last person who saw her alive."

I was frankly a bit on thin ice here, as far as confidentiality is concerned. My role as attorney for the estate probably didn't mean that anything Joe and I talked about was under the protective wings of confidentiality. I was taking I suppose some slight risk, but I was almost positive I was not about to hear a confession of murder or anything along those lines.

At any rate, Joe folded. I often play that confidentiality card. Whether it was valid or not. It often had a marvelous effect. Or maybe he simply hated to tell a pack of lies. "OK, I was there, I admit it," he said. "I drove down that night, to see her, and I did see her. We, well, let's say we had a conversation."

"Then why didn't you tell me about this? Why did you lie? You said you never met your grandmother. Now you tell me you did."

"I'm really sorry. I really am. But I promised... she asked me to say these things. My grandmother. It was her idea for me to come. She called me, she said she wanted to see me. She said, don't tell anybody, ever, about this. Lie about it if necessary. It's nobody's business but ours."

"Didn't you think that was a bit, well, weird?"

"I did. But I thought, maybe she's ashamed, she doesn't want anybody to know; about me, that is. After all, my dad was illegitimate. So was I. In her day, when she was young, that was considered really awful, wasn't it? Probably she kept all this stuff a secret all this time. I know she did. Now, late in her life, here comes this kid, this living proof of... what she did. So

I thought she still didn't want anybody to know. It's too pain-ful. That's what I figured. And she was an old woman, and she was my grandmother. I felt I had to respect her wishes."

"OK. So you came down?"

"I did. I drove down after dinner. The traffic was pretty bad, you know, on the bridge. The Bay Bridge I mean. I parked the car and rang the bell; she answered, and asked me to come upstairs with her. She had a kind of study there, a little room with a desk and a couple of chairs and a sofa. We sat for a while and talked. She asked me if I wanted something, coffee or something, and I said no. It was... kind of weird. For both of us. You can understand that. I mean, she was my grandmoth-er, but I never laid eyes on her before. I didn't know, should I hug her, that sort of thing. Anyway, it was weird, as I said. For her too, I think. She was a stranger to me, and I was a stranger to her.

"She asked me how much I knew about my father, and I said I knew almost nothing, which was the truth. She said she didn't know very much herself. She said he was dead. She said he had turned out very badly, and that this was something that hurt her inside, hurt her terribly. She felt it was, in a way, her fault—that if she had kept him and brought him up herself, took care of him, he might have turned out some other way. But in those days, she said, it just wasn't possible. She said her mother and sister, and her brothers, they all put a lot of pres-sure on her—they insisted she had to give up the baby. So she did.

"And she said, she thought I was lucky, I got put in a good home, with good people. I agreed, I said I knew I was lucky. She asked me a bunch of questions about my mother, what was she like, and that sort of thing. She asked if my mom had a family. And I said, not really, her parents were dead, and she had no brothers and sisters, and I said that she—Mrs. Win-gate—was the first blood relative I ever really met, except for my mother. And... well, she started to cry, and she said would I mind, she wanted to give me a hug, and I said no, of course not, I wouldn't mind. Up to that point, we had been, well, pretty formal, I was embarrassed, actually. As I told you, Mr. May, it was a pretty weird feeling, you know, to meet your grandmother for the first time and... well, let's leave it at that: it was weird."

I said I thought I understood. He continued: "But, you know, I was kind of happy, too, about this whole business. She was really impressive, somehow—I can't explain it, but there was something about her. She was old, but she wasn't an old lady, if you know what I mean. She was so... *alive*. Kind of awesome. But sad, too. There was something that seemed to be... haunting her."

"Haunting her? What do you mean?"

"Well, maybe I wouldn't have thought so, if she hadn't said some funny things or acted so mysterious. She warned me again: never tell anybody you were here, never mention my name to anybody, and don't tell people about our relationship, not now anyway. And I said, of course, I'll do what you want, but she could tell by my face that I thought this was, well, painful. So she took me by the shoulder and she said: Listen, Joe. You think I'm ashamed of you. I'm not ashamed of you. I'm proud of you. If I could, I would tell the whole world about you, I'd adopt you, I'd do anything for you. But it can't be. I can't explain why. I wouldn't want anything or anybody to hurt you. Trust me and do it my way."

"She said that? She talked about somebody maybe... *hurting* you?"

"Those were her words."

"And... you don't know what she meant by that?"

"No idea. She never explained. I was hoping maybe *you'd* know. Maybe you could explain it to me. But... I couldn't ask you—I made that promise, not to tell anybody. Believe me, I've thought about it a lot."

17

In fact, I had no information to give Joe. None at all. These remarks, these cryptic sayings, they were consistent with things Barbara told me, the first time we talked about the subject. Harriet Wingate, in the last weeks of her life, was deathly afraid of something or somebody. She was afraid for herself, and apparently for Joe Pangea too, or at least it seemed that way. But who was she afraid of? Tommy? That was Barbara's theory. I just couldn't accept that. It was too ridiculous. And yet... who else?

I could imagine being afraid of Vincent Fosco. That made sense. But he had been dead for a year. Dead and gone. Skunks and raccoons had been nibbling at his carcass: the police had to identify him through his teeth. And what possible connection did he have with Harriet? Or with Tommy, for that matter?

Meanwhile, Joe went on talking. "Mrs. Wingate, I mean, my grandmother, she said, she had something else to talk to me about. That's when she showed me the will."

"The copy?"

"No, not the copy. She showed me a document, it looked like the original, you know, signed and everything. She showed it to me, and she explained that it was a new will, it was mostly like the old will, but she wanted me to have some money, to help me with college and that sort of thing. I said, I really don't need the money, my folks are doing OK. She said well, I want you to have it. Then she gave me an envelope, this sealed envelope, and she said: this is a copy of the will. You keep it, it might be useful."

"So you lied to me, when you said she mailed it to you."

"Yes."

"And why did you make up that story?"

"It was my grandmother's story. She told me to tell people that I got it in the mail, if anybody asked."

"And the original, what happened to it?"

"Well, I don't really know. She said I'm going to put the original in a safe place. In the house. I'm going to tell you where, too. And she showed me a desk in her study, pretty ordinary desk, with a bunch of drawers. She took a key and unlocked one of the drawers, and she put the document in it. She said, this is where I keep my valuable papers and things, I don't use safe deposit boxes. Well, I've got some stock certificates, but that's all. Otherwise, I like to have things here where I can look at them and change my mind if I feel like it."

"And... she put the original in that drawer?"

"She did. And then she locked the drawer."

"What did she do with the key?"

"Put it in her purse, I think. I don't really remember."

But I remembered the locked drawer very well. It was one of the first things we searched, looking for the will. Barbara had a key. I told you that already.

And of course there was no will in the drawer when we opened it. Some time between Harriet's conversation with Joe Pangea—assuming he was telling the truth—and the day we looked in the house, which was less than twenty-four hours after Harriet died, somebody took that will out of the drawer.

It could have been Harriet herself. That was certainly possible. Took it out and tore it up. Unlikely, but possible. If she did this, it had to be almost immediately after Joe Pangea left. Because pretty soon she was dead.

If not Harriet Wingate, then who? Sophie, maybe. She was in the house, and by her own admission, she was there after Joe had left. But... Harriet was also in the house at that point. And was presumably still alive.

My mind filled with wild thoughts: Sophie could have nipped upstairs, killed Harriet Wingate, taken the key out of the purse and filched the will.

But why? I could see a motive for killing Harriet—then Tommy would get all that money, and right away. But why take the will? It left plenty of money to Tommy. Was it worth destroying it, just because it also gave Joe Pangea $75,000? That was a small amount of money, considering the size of Harriet's estate. And Sophie must have known that. She was counting on getting her hands on millions. $75,000 was lunch money.

No, this just didn't make sense. Anyway, if Sophie killed Harriet, why did she do it with poison?

The poison point was really troublesome. Maybe I was thinking along the wrong lines. I was picturing somebody handing Harriet a cup of something full of poison, or forcing it down her throat. But there had been no sign of a struggle.

Maybe somebody poisoned her earlier, somehow; maybe it was one of those poisons that don't take effect for a while. I know nothing whatsoever about poison. As I said, mystery stories are full of poisons. In Agatha Christie, something called chloral hydrate is at the root of a lot of murders. I hope I've got the name right. They poison people with it. I have no idea what it is. The books are always talking about a colorless, odorless, and tasteless poison. Was that chloral hydrate? I had no idea. In this case, the poisoning really seemed weird. Maybe Harriet took the poison herself. But why? Anyway, she left no note or any indication. Besides, one thing we knew: she was clearly afraid of something or somebody. Was she so frightened she decided to end it all?

Sophie and the will: if she took the will and destroyed it, that would explain why she tore up Tommy's holographic will. It had an earlier date, naturally. And the later will might have revoked the earlier will. Undoubtedly it said so. But I really didn't credit Sophie with sophisticated knowledge of California rules about wills and the like. All in all nothing yet made sense to me.

I had been quiet for a while, thinking these thoughts. Joe and I were still sitting on a bench in San Mateo, even though my thoughts had gone miles and miles away. Joe interrupted my reverie: "Mr. May?"

"...yes?"

"You aren't saying anything."

I said, "Sorry, Joe. I was thinking. This whole business, and you don't know the half of it, but it's getting to me. I can't figure anything out. Nothing makes sense, somehow. Anyway, let's get back to you. After she gave you this envelope, you went out, got into your car and went home, is that right?"

"Well, not exactly," he said. "It's a long drive, and I don't come down the peninsula very often. I've got a friend, from high school, he goes to Stanford. He lives in a dorm, a big dorm, on the campus. Florence Moore Hall I think it's called. I told him I was coming down, and he said, let's get together. So I went over and spent some time with him. We had a pizza, and I sat in his room, and we talked about school and courses and we traded impressions of our schools, and we talked about old times, you know, that sort of thing. And then... he said he had to study, and I said, me too, I've got to go. But instead of driving home, I did something pretty weird. It was pretty late by then—I think it was about one o'clock, maybe later... but instead of going straight home, I drove back to my grandmother's house."

"You did what?"

"I drove back to her house. I don't know why. I wasn't going to go in, nothing like that. It was too late. I was sure she was asleep. I mean, it was the middle of the night. I just... wanted to go back and look at the house, and think. I can't explain it. It was... well, I had all these emotions. You know, when you're adopted, and—I guess you can't know, you're probably not adopted—but, I mean, all these feelings... Anyway, I just felt like sitting there and thinking, and looking at the house. My grandmother's house. And that's what I did.

"There was a small light on upstairs. I didn't think anything of it. Lots of people leave lights on, even when they're asleep. My dad's aunt does that, when she comes to visit. His aunt comes and visits us, she's about 80, getting frail. She's afraid of falling down. She always leaves a light on in the bathroom.

"Anyway, there was a light on in the house. I was sitting there in the dark in my car, just trying to sort things out. Then I saw somebody come out the door."

"You saw somebody come out the door?"

"Yes. I kind of scrunched down in the seat, I was afraid he could see me...."

"You said 'he.' It was a man?"

"Yes. I mean, that's what I thought...."

"Young or old?"

"I couldn't see. It was dark. Just a shape, really."

"Tall or short."

"Medium. I really don't know."

"And you have no idea who it was?"

"No idea."

"Didn't you think it was... funny? I mean, somebody coming out of the house, that late at night?"

"I guess. But you know, it could have been somebody who lived there.... I mean, I didn't know anything about my grandmother, her way of life, any of that. At the time, I didn't even know she was married. Married to some guy not much older than I was. Hey, that was a shocker when I found out. Anyway, I thought it was peculiar, seeing this guy come out of the house, but not all that strange; I didn't really think much about it. I just started my car and drove home."

"And the man: what did he do? Did you see?"

"No... I think he went around the corner. I didn't see him get in his car, but he must have."

"Did you notice *anything* about him? The way he walked, or anything? Like: did he limp, or... *anything*?"

"Nothing. Not really. It was dark, like I said, and I was in a hurry to get out of there. I didn't want anybody seeing me, you know, sitting in a car outside somebody's house. So... like I said, I just drove home."

A man... coming out of Harriet's house. In the middle of the night. This was important. And strange. Could it have been Tommy? If so, what was he doing there at that hour? Harriet Wingate was already dead by then. Or maybe not. Maybe the man had killed her. I know Barbara was convinced that Tommy was violent, even a killer. Of course, I doubted that.

I was lost in my reveries again. Joe brought me back to reality. "Mr. May, I've got to go now," he said. "I've got to get back."

"Of course, Joe," I said.

"I'm sorry I lied to you."

I told him I understood. I shook his hand. He got in his car and drove off.

I watched him drive down the street. I suppose you would have to consider him a suspect. After all, he was in the house that night; he admitted it. And he admitted, too, that he had gone back later.

Was *he* telling the truth? I couldn't be sure of anybody. Lots of people in this miserable affair seemed to be lying to me.

Still, in the back of my mind, I was forming an idea.

Don't get me wrong. I'm not a detective. I'm not the least bit like the characters in detective stories, you know, Miss Marple or Kelsey Milhone or Sam Spade. They get these flashes of brilliant inspiration. Sherlock Holmes used to look at a dog turd or something and come up with a description of the dog's owner and whether he was married or single and how tall he was and the color of his hair, not to mention the identity of the culprit in the case and God knows what else. I don't have these waves of insight. I got an idea, not because I'm a born sleuth, but because... well, because I do have one trait a detective is supposed to have: a suspicious mind. Lawyers also have suspicious minds. If they don't, they can't survive.

As I said, I was beginning to get a vague idea about Harriet's death. Believe me, it wasn't a stroke of genius, but instead... well, never mind. There were still a fair number of loose ends. Among the biggest and loosest of these was the death of Vincent Fosco. I had no idea who he even *was*, let alone why it mattered who he was. Could it be that the murder of Vincent

Fosco was completely unrelated to the murder of Harriet Wingate? I suppose that was possible, but somehow I doubted it. The police, I imagined, were hard at work trying to solve that case. And they seemed to think poor Tommy Wingate was the man they were after, but I had no way of finding out what the police were up to and why. The closest I could come was to talk to Barbara, who seemed to have some sort of pipeline to the investigation. But Barbara was blinded by prejudice; she was an inveterate Tommy-hater, and I wanted to avoid an argument with her, though it was bound to occur.

The second best thing was to talk to her sister Karen. Karen was younger than Barbara, I knew her less well, but she was more reasonable, shall we say. Certainly on the issue of Tommy. So I got on the phone, rang her up, and asked if I could come to see her.

"What about?"

"Oh... the estate," I said.

"The estate. Should I ask Barbara to join us?"

"Karen, don't take this the wrong way, but I'd rather not have Barbara at this point. I need to talk to you alone, if that's OK. Don't mention it to your sister. I'll... I'll fill her in later. I promise."

The slight air of intrigue obviously fascinated her; and she agreed. "Come over for coffee tonight, OK?" she said. "Barbara is going to the opera with some friend of hers. I'm not going. They offered me a ticket, but I turned it down. It's five hours of Wagner. It's *Siegfried*. I can't sit for five hours listening to people shrieking on the stage."

"I'll see you at eight."

Of course, in my eagerness to play Mr. Detective, I had forgotten to tell Celia I was going out that night. She wasn't happy when I told her, at dinner, that I would be visiting a client. It wasn't the fact that I'd be gone; it was the fact that I hadn't told her beforehand. She was disappointed. "I was hoping we could take in a movie. I don't know why you just spring these things on me. *I* never make plans without consulting *you*."

She was right about that. A hundred percent right. And I should have admitted it. But husbands never admit they are wrong. Never. It's a genetic thing with men. Married men at least. Marriage stimulates this gene to become operational; and from the date of the marriage on, men never can admit they were wrong. So I left the house under a mild sort of cloud.

But it wasn't acrimonious. The fact is, Celia and I really love each other, the way people do who stay married a long time, and whose lives are complete entwined in each other. Of course, I know that sometimes with the passage of time, the other thing happens: two people come to hate each other's guts. That is all too frequent, I'm afraid. I have many clients like that.

But that's not us, no way. We're still in love. It's a low-key, mature kind of love, but it *is* love. Young couples, the ones who can't stay away from each other for a minute, and who screw three times a day, have trouble understanding this kind of love. But believe me, it's real.

At a quarter to eight, I left the house and drove to Karen's. Celia had already forgotten she was annoyed.

18

Karen lived in a condominium in Palo Alto, not too far from her sister—and not far from Harriet's house as well. It was an apartment complex, about the same size as the one Tommy lived in, but much more upscale. It was a few blocks from University Avenue, which is more or less Palo Alto's Main Street, as I think I told you. This meant you were within walking distance of a dozen coffee houses, a Burmese restaurant, some banks, a jewelry store, and many, many shops selling things nobody needs, and at very high prices.

Karen's condo was small but neat. Karen too was small but neat. She was short, thin, about 50 years old, with a somewhat pinched face; her hair was long and very black. In some ways she looked like an older version of Sophie, but without the bangles and the countercultural look.

"Coffee, Frank?"

I said sure. She went into the kitchen, and came out fairly soon with a tray, two cups, and a pot of steaming coffee. Her coffee was a lot better than Sophie's. She also put out some cake; white, with chocolate icing. I resisted taking some for at least two minutes. Karen, I noticed, did not indulge.

"Karen, I need some help," I said, when I was through with the cake.

"Whatever I can do, Frank."

"I don't know where to start," I said. "This thing is such a mess. Your aunt's estate, I mean. As things now stand, there's this torn will... that's the only one we've actually got on hand; so I filed it with the probate court. You know that, don't you?"

She nodded.

"The other wills," I said, "well, who knows what happened to them. But, in any event, the bottom line is this: so far, you, Barbara, and Tommy will share the estate."

"I know that too," she said.

"But: and here's the complication. Tommy. If... well, if he was responsible for your aunt's death; if he killed her...."

"You can't believe that, Frank."

"Not for a minute, Karen. Really, I don't. But your sister...."

"Oh, Barbara's completely irrational on the subject," Karen said. "She just doesn't *know* Tommy. I do."

I wondered just how and why she knew him. But I didn't pursue this subject. "I want you to tell me about Tommy," I said. "If he did have a role in this, then you and Barbara share the estate, and he gets cut out."

"I don't want that," she said.

"Does Barbara?"

Karen said: "She does. Not for the money, no. We're not greedy people. It's... well, it's because she hates the poor guy. She's convinced he's no good, she thinks he's been abusive— you saw how she behaved, with that doctor—and she thinks it would be a crime if he got a cent out of poor Harriet's estate."

"Barbara has some sort of connection with the police? I mean, she knows things, about the investigation and all that: isn't that true?"

"I think so."

"And does she talk to you?"

"Yes. At least it seems that way," Karen said. "Maybe she doesn't tell me everything. Things have been a bit strained between us lately, but, yes, she tells me things."

"I'll tell you what I'm after," I said. "First of all: just general information. For instance, who on earth was Vincent Fosco? And why do they think Tommy had something to do with Fosco? Why do they think Tommy killed him? I don't have a clue."

Karen sipped her coffee slowly. "I know a little bit, not too much. Things I heard from Barbara. This Fosco, he was some kind of gangster. He had a long criminal record; and he was a fugitive from justice, I think. I guess Tommy was supposed to be mixed up in something, some crime, something Fosco was involved in."

"When was this? I mean, Tommy's involvement."

"Not too recent. It was before he came to live with Aunt Harriet. That's about all I know. Oh yes: the police found some sort of evidence, when they found the body. I don't know what this was. But whatever it was, they traced it to Tommy. At least that's what they say."

"You're sure about that? You say they found some kind of evidence. Could it be fingerprints?"

I realized immediately how stupid this sounded. She said, "Fingerprints? Frank, this was a year-old corpse, I don't even know how they identified it, and I don't want to know, it's too disgusting to think about. By the teeth, I suppose."

"But what connected the body to Tommy? Do you know?"

"I'm not sure. Barbara hinted that it might have been a gun, buried with the body. But... that's all I can tell you."

"Tommy had a gun?" Now I didn't feel so stupid about my fingerprints question; maybe a gun had prints on it.

"Not that I ever knew about, but I suppose it's possible. Lots of people have guns."

"And this gun... it was the murder weapon?"

"I suppose so, Frank. Really, you'd have to ask Barbara or the police. I just couldn't tell you."

"OK, you said Tommy may have been mixed up with this guy, this Fosco person, and you said 'from before.' From before he came to live with Harriet. But where was that? Where did Tommy come from? Do you know anything about him?"

She said: "Well, that's the funny part. I just don't know. Tommy appeared, out of the blue, sort of like magic. It was, oh, maybe three years ago. He started out doing yard work for Aunt Harriet, and that sort of thing. Odd jobs. I thought he was just somebody she hired, a kind of helper around her house, and that somehow she took a liking to him from the very start. She... no, I don't want to give the wrong impression. It wasn't romantic. It was more grandmotherly, you know what I mean? She wanted to help him. And he was always polite. Look: I liked him too."

"Did he have a *name*? Nowadays he calls himself Tommy Wingate."

"Aunt Harriet insisted on that. It was her idea. Of course, he had a name. Said it was Smith, if you believe him. I suppose there are lots of people who are actually named Smith, but somehow I don't think Tommy was one of those people, I think it was a made-up name. Anyway, Aunt Harriet said, we're going to call you Tommy Wingate. Barbara nearly had a fit when she heard this: she thought Aunt Harriet had lost her mind."

"And... he lived in her house?"

"From the start. I think I told you all this already. He had a room in the attic. Then she moved him into a nicer room. They were tight as can be. Tommy... you know, he's a rather limited person. I mean, the poor guy never had much of a chance to get an education. But he and Harriet, they became great friends. I guess he was company for her. She lived alone, after all. Then there was Tommy, young, good-looking, and really pretty polite and helpful to her. Still, I was amazed when they got married."

"You had no clue it was going to happen?"

"Well, funny things had been going on. Like that incident when the doctor came. Barbara, well, you know this, she was convinced Tommy was beating Aunt Harriet. Elder abuse, she said. I told her it was preposterous. Well, you've met Tommy. You know it *was* preposterous. But *something* was going on. She got herself a burglar alarm, for instance. Barbara said she's afraid of Tommy. I said nonsense. He's *inside* the house; what good does it do to have a burglar alarm?"

A burglar alarm. I hadn't realized the house *had* a burglar alarm. I thought about the night Harriet Wingate died. If there was a burglar alarm, did Sophie know about it? If she did, did she turn it off? Presumably, if she did, she must have known how, must have known the code.

I asked for more information about the burglar alarm. "Is it still there?"

"As far as I know."

"What kind is it?"

"What kinds are there? I don't know anything about burglar alarms. I don't have one. I suppose it was nothing special. The usual kind? It makes a horrendous noise if you forget to turn it off when you come in. And it sends some kind of signal to the alarm company, or to the police, I don't know, one of the two."

"Is there a code, or a password?"

"Oh, yes."

"Who knew the code?"

"Barbara and I. Tommy, I guess. I wouldn't imagine anybody else would know."

Well, Sophie might have known, I thought. She could have wormed the code out of Tommy or simply watched him use it. That wouldn't have been much of a problem. But what about that other man, the one Joe saw, late at night, coming out of the house? What was he doing there? How did he get in? And did *he* know the code? Was Harriet Wingate dead or alive when he arrived? And when he left?

Karen had not given me much information—not really. But, oddly enough, I felt that things were starting to come together. It wasn't as if I was conducting an investigation. It was just that somehow I attracted information. Facts had a funny habit of coming at me even when I wasn't looking for them.

For example, a few days later, I found a long letter from Joe waiting for me at the office.

"Dear Mr. May," it said. "It's easier for me to write this in a letter than to tell you in person. It's something I have to admit I left out of the story when I talked to you.

"I don't know how you knew I had visited my grandmother that night. I guess I don't want to know. Anyway, I haven't heard anything from the police. They haven't questioned me, and I hope they don't know I exist. If so, I'd like to keep it that way.

"What I want to tell you now has nothing to do with that visit. Not directly, at least. It has to do with me, and I wanted you to know about it. Maybe it'll help you understand me a bit better.

"I guess, like a lot of adopted kids, I always had this gnawing hunger inside, I wanted to know more. As I told you, I've been very lucky, my adoptive dad is great. I couldn't have gotten anything better, and I love him. And I hope I haven't been a disappointment to my parents. I try not to be. And I always tell him, you're my real dad, and I don't want anybody else and so on. But I just felt I had to know more about my biological father.

"I don't know where my mother met my father, Hendricks. She got pregnant. They never married. Hendricks deserted her almost the minute I was born. My birth mom was always a good person, but she had had a difficult childhood. Somehow she had gotten mixed up with a really rotten guy. After I was born, she tried to straighten out her life, and she did straighten it out, after she married my dad—I mean my adoptive dad.

"From then on, she was on the right path. But my father, my birth father, well, that was a different story. One thing, though, he was easy to trace once I had his name and once I set my mind to it. Only what I found out was truly horrible.

"OK, so he was a criminal, I think I could have handled that pretty easily. But he was not just an ordinary criminal. He was vicious, brutal, a real psychopath. Can you imagine what it feels like to find out something like that? That your real father was a psychopathic killer? Because that's what he was. He had a prison record a yard long. He killed another kid when he was still a juvenile. He killed an inmate in San Quentin in some kind of fight. He was put on trial for murder. He said it was self-defense, and I guess the jury believed him. So he got off, that time.

"It was the way he died that was the most upsetting thing for me, the most horrifying. He was on some kind of a crime spree. He had escaped from prison, in Arizona—that's where he was at the time, for some reason. He was in for a long term, for armed robbery, aggravated assault, other stuff. He broke out and went right back to armed robbery. He got connected with another man, somebody equally awful, and a woman and her son, about 16 years old. The woman was somebody I guess he had been living with, or was currently living with, or something, and the kid was hers from some other guy. So my dad, along with the two of them, and one of his prison buddies, set out to rob some store, and they took the money and beat up the clerk, and then they ran away. Then their car broke down on a side road outside of Tucson, I think it was. They made the kid and the woman flag down a car, it was a lonely road, not many cars, but finally somebody stopped—it was late at night —and of course, they flagged them down because they wanted to steal the car.

"The people in it—there were four people, a young married couple and their two kids—and they were going somewhere, I don't know where. It was just their luck that they were on this road at that precise time, that's what life is like. Anyway, they saw the woman and her son and they stopped, thinking they were going to help out some people in distress. My dad forced them out of the car at gunpoint, and he marched them off the road. He and the other guy were debating what to do with them, and the woman and the kid were there too. And the upshot was, my dad and his buddy, they shot the four of them, the people who had been in the car, they shot them in cold blood just like that—I guess because they had seen their faces and could identify them. They left the four of them for dead lying in their own blood at the side of the road.

"The couple and one of the kids really were dead, but one of the children, a girl, was just unconscious. She survived. It was sort of a miracle. Anyway, she lived to tell the tale, and the police were searching for my dad anyway because of the prison break. They caught up with my dad and his accomplices, they were in a kind of cabin in the desert, holed up there. There was a gunfight, the police surrounded the cabin, there was a lot of shooting. Two cops were injured and my dad was killed. The other three people got away, or maybe they weren't there in the first place, I don't know. As far as I can tell, the police never caught them.

"I found all this out by reading newspaper reports online —it was a big story, at least in Arizona—three people killed, and all the gory details. As you can imagine, it was just devastating for me. This was what I came from, this was the guy who was my father. These are the genes I carry around inside of me. For days I couldn't think of anything else. I was really depressed, and I'm not easily depressed, I'm basically a happy guy. I was already a student at Berkeley when I found all this out, and I flew home for a few days because I just couldn't take it. Mom and Dad were terrific, and told me over and over again that there's nothing to be ashamed of, I'm my own person. And what my father did, you don't inherit it. I ended up still really upset but I thought I could handle it.

"So I hope you'll understand why meeting my grand-mother was so important to me. When I met her I found out that she was a normal person, somebody decent, law-abiding, respected in the community. I wanted to feel that I wasn't the product of a long line of psychopaths. I know that in a way it's ridiculous to think that there's some sort of criminal gene, something you inherit. All this genetic stuff is way overdone—I know it's controversial, all that nature versus nurture contro-versy. But I *have* to believe there's nothing to the idea that this kind of criminal stuff goes down from parent to child. You can see why. It was a comfort to me, to know that maybe it was my father who was the exception, not the rule. That's why I came to see her, and why I just couldn't let go. And now she's dead. You know, it's funny: I only met her once but I'm having a real sad reaction. And I'm terribly sorry about all the lies. I hope you won't think too bad of me.

"One more lie I've got to get off my chest. I told you some weird story about a man calling me, and telling me my grand-mother was dead. There was no such man and no such call. I was ashamed to tell you how I found out she was dead. I drove down here to see her, there was nobody around, and the house was locked up. I began to wonder, was she on a trip? And then I remembered how she seemed scared, how strangely she behaved. And I thought maybe something happened to her. So I checked the local newspapers, and I was shocked to find out she was dead. The very morning after I came to see her, they found her dead, in her bed!

"That made things worse, somehow. I have this real feeling of regret that I didn't get to know her better. I really wish I had.

"And I truly don't care about the money. You have to believe me when I tell you this. I guess you'll never find the will. I don't care. I just hope that it all goes smoothly, the estate and all. And I would like to meet my grandmother's family someday, her nieces. Not now though. I have a feeling they'd resent me, they'd imagine I'm after the money. You told me I really don't have a claim. I don't want to claim anything—I'd like to have a picture of her, maybe. And I do want to get to know my cousins. After all, they're relatives, just like she was."

I read the letter over twice. I found it strangely moving. I felt I had to share it with somebody, but Barbara and Karen weren't the right ones. Not yet, anyway. I did show it to Celia. She said we had to have the boy down for dinner some time. She said she felt sorry for him. The terrible truth about his father. Still he has a lot going for him. He was lucky in some regards: his adoptive father, for one thing. And he was clearly intelligent and stable. Yet I'll be honest: although I told Celia, sure, let's have him for dinner, I didn't mean it. The whole affair, the whole Wingate mess, left a bad taste in my mouth.

I thought a lot about the letter and what it told me. As far as I knew, the police had no idea there was such a person as Joe Pangea, or that he had been at his grandmother's house the night she died. Been inside, and later sat outside, in his car, observing. They would have been particularly interested in the man who came out the front door. Clearly they had no idea that anybody had even been there that night.

These were busy times for me—I had a lot of work to do at the office—but I couldn't resist taking time out whenever I could, to do a little research on my own. I wanted to know more about the late Mr. Hendricks, Joe's father, and Harriet's son.

It wasn't hard to find newspaper articles about Hendricks through Google and in the newspapers. At Stanford, they have a big database of newspapers online. A friend of mine who teaches there helped me get access. There was plenty of material on Hendricks. I found even more through other newspaper files that the library had on microfilm. The Arizona newspapers, for example.

What a miserable life this guy must have led. Miserable and violent.

Joe's letter had been pretty accurate in most regards. His account conformed pretty well to the coverage in the newspapers. But he hadn't bothered to mention exactly *when* these things took place and a few other details as well. I found the actual dates of the crime spree illuminating, to say the least. It all tied together with ideas that were germinating in my head.

I hate microfilm, but it was microfilm or nothing with some of the older newspapers—the ones that were not online. Nobody keeps originals. I always get the reels in backwards the first time I try. That makes me feel like an idiot. Anyway, I made copies of some of the crucial articles. Other material luckily was online and I could print it out.

You know, busy as I was with clients, and a family man with two teenage daughters is pretty busy in other regards, I was clearly obsessed with this case. It *haunted* me. I couldn't get it out of my mind. And, as I said, I was starting to get some ideas. Maybe my imagination was running away with me. But, as you will see, my ideas were far from wrong. Anyway, all of this in due course.

19

About a week or so after I got Joe Pangea's letter, and a few days after my brilliant newspaper research, Barbara called me at the office. There was a note of triumph in her voice. "Frank," she said, "you never believe me, but this time I turned out to be right."

"I *always* believe you, Barbara. Right about what?"

She said, "They arrested Tommy. The police. Charged him with murder."

"Tommy?"

"I said, Tommy. Didn't you hear me, Frank? I said they arrested him, and charged him with murder."

"What murder, Barbara? Was it this Fosco person?"

"Absolutely. And my friend, the one in the department, says they have tons of evidence. Tons. He used that very word. Frank, I knew it all along."

"And... your aunt? Anything about that?"

She said: "Not yet. Oh, I'm sure he had something to do with it. That would be too much of a coincidence, wouldn't it? Tommy killed this Fosco, and somebody *else* killed Aunt Harriet? I don't believe in that kind of coincidence. Oh, that was Tommy all right. But they don't have the evidence. Not yet."

"Barbara, I'll be honest with you. I find all of this pretty hard to believe. I mean, I've *met* Tommy. OK, I suppose I could be wrong about him—"

"You *are* wrong about him."

"OK, it could be. But it seems completely out of character...."

"Out of character? Frank, don't be naïve."

I said, "OK, I won't argue the point. But let's take this Fosco person. He was shot, I guess."

"You guess right."

"And you say Tommy shot him."

"I say it, but that's not important. The important thing is that the *police* say it."

"And you say, they have tons of evidence."

"Tons."

I said, "I don't know the evidence, so I can't comment. You'd have to convince me. I don't see Tommy as a killer. But I suppose it's possible, people get desperate sometimes; maybe it was self-defense."

"Self-defense? On what account?"

"Barbara, how would I know? I know nothing about Fosco. I'm just speculating."

She said: "Frank, don't be stubborn. Would the police arrest somebody innocent? Be serious."

Of course, the police arrest innocent people all the time. But I didn't feel like arguing with a valuable client. "OK, OK," I said. "Anyway, I don't know anything about Fosco. I can't comment on that part. But the idea that Tommy poisoned your aunt? I just can't go along. It's too crazy."

"You'll see," she said. "I've been right so far."

"And... what was his motive? For killing this Fosco guy? What was the reason?"

"I don't know that. Who knows? Maybe they were having an argument. Maybe Fosco had something on him. What do we know about Tommy? Nothing. He was probably a juvenile delinquent. Or worse. The two of them were probably tied up in some racket together. Fosco had a record a mile long, a really vicious criminal, a thug, that's what he was. Maybe Tommy has a record too. The police will figure it out."

"And why would he kill your aunt?"

"Money, Frank: the oldest and strongest motive."

I really didn't want to continue contradicting her; in fact, I thought it was time to give up and end the conversation. "I guess we'll see, Barbara," I said to her.

"We will," she said. "I tell you, Frank, we're near the end of this thing finally."

She was right, as it turned out, but in a way she couldn't possibly suspect. When the police arrested Tommy, they set a process in motion. And the process ended soon enough, in my office of all places.

But of course I didn't know that yet.

Most people who are arrested get out on bail—that is, if they have any money at all or any connections. That's true for most crimes. People accused of murder are usually treated differently. They have to sit in jail until they're tried, unless they're released for lack of evidence.

I was thinking of Tommy, of course, behind bars. I was tempted to go see him, but thought better of it. Instead I picked up the phone and called Karen. I asked her if she wouldn't go visit him. "Talk to the guy," I said to her. "Try to find out what's going on. Who was this Vincent Fosco? And how is Tommy tied up with him?"

Karen said, "I'll go. I was thinking of doing it anyway. Poor Tommy. You don't think he actually killed this Fosco, do you? It's totally out of the question. Not Tommy."

"Karen, I just don't know what to think. I agree with you; it seems so preposterous. But Barbara keeps talking about evidence. She says the police have all kinds of evidence. I don't know what she means; maybe if you talk to Tommy, you'll get some sort of idea."

"Can't we get him out on bail?"

I explained to her why we couldn't. She said, "I just can't think about Tommy in that awful place. The things you read about. The brutality...."

I wondered if Tommy was quite as unused to prison life as Karen seemed to think, but I kept my views to myself. Anyway, Karen did do her duty: she went to visit Tommy in jail. Afterwards, she came to see me in my office. It was a dreadful experience, she said. I suppose she had never visited anybody in jail before. Few of us have.

Basically, she had very little to report. She said Tommy was scared, nervous, and didn't want to talk very much. He also reported that "Mr. Thom did want him to say anything to anybody. He made me promise."

"Well, it's pretty good advice, generally speaking," I said.

"But Barbara seems to know a great deal," Karen told me. "She said she thinks there were witnesses... people who identified Tommy."

"Identified Tommy? As what? A witness? Somebody saw him kill Vincent Fosco?"

"Not exactly. But this young couple saw him coming out of the woods, and getting into a car. It was in the middle of the night. He was dressed in old clothes, looked very dirty, and was carrying a shovel. This couple was parked there in the woods, in their own car...."

"What were they doing there?"

"Frank, don't be a baby. What do you think they were doing there? The usual thing a young couple does when they think nobody is around. But these two, they can't be sure about the date. They didn't say anything at the time, because, after all, it's not a crime to be in the woods at night with a shovel. Maybe they were a little embarrassed and didn't want to be seen. They said they think this person didn't see them. He got into a car. They thought maybe somebody else was sitting in the car, too, but they weren't sure."

"And why did they come forward now?"

"Because a body was found buried in the woods. They read about it in the paper, and they realized, the spot where the body was found was... well, near where they were parked. So they went to the police, and told their story. That's as much as I know. I mean, as much as Barbara knows."

"It was night-time, you said?"

"Yes. Middle of the night."

"So how could they identify Tommy?"

"Well, this is the story, as Barbara tells it. They didn't actually identify him. All they can say is that it was a young guy, light colored hair, tied in a ponytail. They can't say for sure it *was* Tommy, but the description fits."

"And the date? How do we know when this Fosco guy died?"

"We don't. They don't. It's all approximate. But the time, the place... at the very least, it isn't inconsistent."

"But, Karen, what led the police to Tommy in the first place? I can't believe they started looking for a young man with a ponytail. There are zillions of them."

"I don't know. But there must have been something."

The something turned out to be extremely alarming. I got the news from Barbara herself, and she was positively crowing: "Frank, now will you believe me? They've charged Tommy with three more murders."

"*Three*? You mean not just Harriet?"

She said, "Not Aunt Harriet at all. Three other people. In Arizona, I think it was. Years ago. And his accomplice at that time was Vincent Fosco! So they were part of a gang or something like that. Anyway, now, for some reason, Tommy must have decided he was going to get rid of Fosco too. Maybe they had a fight about money. Who knows?"

"Did you say, Arizona?"

"Yes. Near Phoenix. I don't know any details."

Arizona. Of course. It couldn't be just a coincidence. I remembered Joe Pangea's letter: the horrifying story of how his father died. That was in Arizona. And there were three other people present during the crime. One was a woman—he had no idea who she was—and then there was a man, and a boy of about 16 or so. Could it be that the boy was Tommy? And could the man have been... Vincent Fosco?

And did that mean that I *was* in fact all wrong about Tommy: that he was involved in some really heavy, murderous stuff? People are mysterious, I grant you that: we think we know somebody, and then it turns out we don't. Some nice CPA, "so friendly, so polite, that's what the neighbors all say" and it turns out he's got whips and chains in a secret room in the basement or worse yet, maybe parts of dead bodies in his freezer. I was still having trouble seeing Tommy in this role, Tommy the serial killer. Of course, it all made sense if you approached it in Barbara's terms. Maybe Fosco turned up and demanded something from Tommy, or maybe they had a falling out. That could be a motive.

"So you see," Barbara went on, "I was right all along. And this means he doesn't get the money, right?"

"Not so fast," I said, "you know, it doesn't matter whether Tommy killed Vincent Fosco, he could have killed a whole platoon of people for that matter; he still has the right to inherit money from his wife."

"You told me otherwise."

"I didn't, Barbara. I told you he couldn't inherit if he killed *Harriet*. Killing Fosco and two other people doesn't count."

"He did kill her," she said. "They haven't charged him with it yet, but they will, believe me. It's only a question of time."

"Maybe, Barbara. Maybe. But meanwhile, I haven't got any choice in the matter. You haven't got any choice, either, since you're the executor. So far, we have to treat Tommy as an heir. Which he is."

"I think that's ridiculous," she said. "You mean if I leave money to somebody, and he turns out to be a mass murderer, he still gets my money?"

"Actually, yes," I said. "If you want to leave your money to a mass murderer, there's nothing to prevent you. As long as he didn't mass-murder *you*."

"What if you didn't *know* he was a murderer?"

"Makes no difference," I said, though I wasn't *that* sure I was right. Anyway, at that point I had to listen to a speech about how stupid these rules were, how immoral, and so on. I've heard that speech from plenty of clients before, about lots of other rules.

I interrupted her finally, and said, "Well, Barbara, I don't disagree, but the law is the law. Still, if you're right, then I guess they'll find something to tie Tommy to the death of Harriet, and then we won't have a problem. But until then, we just have to do it this way."

She went on and on. I hardly listened: I was getting quite sick of all this. Sick of the squabbling and the endless trouble from the estate of Harriet Wingate. Was it even worth the fee?

Actually, it was. An estate that large would generate a wonderful pile of money. I don't get estates the size of Harriet's very often. In fact, I never do.

A lawyer's time is his money. That's an old cliché. But it's true. Not only did I expect to do well on this estate, but originally I thought there would be very little work. Harriet's affairs had been, as I knew, in very good order. Financially at least. She had a competent accountant, her investments were straightforward... it should have been apple pie.

It had turned out, of course, to be nothing of the sort, not apple pie at all. More like rhubarb. There was the mess with all those wills, and then came Barbara's suspicions. Suspicions which turned out to be right. And if, in addition to all these complications, Tommy was actually charged with murdering Harriet, I could see headache after headache; and the estate might turn out not to be not quite so profitable after all.

It had already eaten up far more of my time than I ever dreamed it would.

So what was the solution? Easy. I had to solve the case. It was as simple as that. I had to figure out who killed Harriet Wingate. I had to use the "leetle gray cells," as Hercule Poirot would put it. I had to sit down, put two and two and two and two together, and come up with an answer.

So I sat down. Then I stood up. Then I walked around. Then I sat on a bench in the park. Then I walked about some more. The little gray cells refused to cooperate.

Let's face it. I wasn't Hercule Poirot. I wasn't Lord Peter Wimsey. I wasn't anybody of that sort. I was Frank May, member of the California bar. I had theories, I had ideas. But all my theories had holes in them. The Wingate affair fascinated me, and repelled me at the same time. Was I going to find a way to solve the case? Was there a way out? I had trouble seeing it. And yet....

In the event, it didn't matter. In this case, there was a consistent pattern of events: everybody came to *me*. They called, they phoned, they dropped in, and everything I learned, I got in a passive way, through listening. The same was true of the solution. It walked in the door of my office, and told me what I wanted to know—what everybody wanted to know. The whole mystery got solved, as it turned out, without too much work from my little gray cells. Or anybody else's gray cells, for that matter.

20

In the short run, I was baffled. Who killed Aunt Harriet? Who killed Vincent Fosco, and why? What did Tommy have to do with all this? I had a thought, but I needed more information, and I didn't know who to turn to.

Except one rather dubious source. But I was shameless by now. I picked up the phone and called Tommy's apartment. Sophie answered, in a rather sharp voice and said, "Who is it?"

"It's me, Sophie. Frank May. I've got to talk to you."

She asked what it was all about. "Well, Tommy, for one thing."

"He's in jail."

"I know that... I'd like to help him. "

She said, "Why? What's it to you?"

I said, "Well, I like Tommy, for one thing...."

"Good for you."

"And, for another thing, I've got professional reasons. You know I'm representing the estate. And Harriet's affairs, well, they'll remain a mess until something gets resolved. Can I come see you?"

"Why?"

I said, "I just want to ask you some questions. About Tommy. Maybe you can give me some information."

She said, "I told you too much last time."

"That was before."

"Look, I talked to the police. For hours. I don't feel like talking any more. I've done all the talking I feel like doing."

I said, "I'll be right over."

She hung up the phone.

I drove as fast as I could to Sophie's place. I was hoping against hope she would still be there and that she'd let me in. And, in fact, when I rang the bell, she came to the door and opened it. "I knew it was you," she said, somewhat sourly.

The place was a bigger mess than ever. Dirty dishes were piled higher in the kitchen sink. There was a funny smell in the air; maybe it was pot, maybe something else, I'm not sure. There were visible dust balls under the sofa. This Sophie was no housekeeper But I knew that already. The door to the bedroom was open. The bed was unmade. I noticed she had a suitcase open on the bed, and some rumpled clothes had been piled inside of the suitcase.

"Going somewhere?" I asked her.

She didn't even have the courtesy to ask me to sit down. Her hair looked even longer and stragglier than before, and it needed a good combing and brushing. She was barefoot. "Yeah, I'm going somewhere," she said.

"Could I ask where?"

"You could ask. But I wouldn't answer."

I said, "Sophie, I know it's been hard on you...."

"*What's* been hard on me?"

"This... this whole thing. Tommy getting arrested...."

"I couldn't care less."

"He's your boyfriend," I said. I could have added: you have sex with him. Doesn't that give you some sort of bond? But maybe it didn't.

"*Was* my boyfriend," she said. "I'm splitting, if you must know."

"But... he needs your help," I said. The minute I said it, I knew it was a stupid thing to say. She just laughed. I said, "Does Tommy know you're going?"

"No, he doesn't. But he wouldn't care either. This thing wasn't going anywhere. Did you know, the old hag tried to break us up? Harriet. She really worked on him, to get rid of me."

"Was she... jealous?"

"Oh, grow up, will you? Jealous of what? No: she told him I was no good. She said I was only after the money. She was right, of course. It's all I wanted, the money. I didn't *mind* Tommy; he was OK. But the money, that's what I was after."

"Well, he still might get the money," I said weakly.

"'Might' isn't good enough for me. It just isn't worth it, even though the old bitch is dead. They'll stick him with a murder charge, and either he won't get a dime in the end, or, if he gets it, the whole thing will go to lawyers. To people like you."

I grabbed her by the arm. I felt desperate. "Sophie, you've got to talk to me."

"Why? I don't owe you anything. I'm just sick of all this. I don't need it. Cops, detectives, even a reporter from some two-bit local newspaper; do you know, the cops came with a search warrant, they turned the house upside down? I'm out of here."

"Just tell me about Tommy.... I want to know everything you know about him?"

"Everything what? The size of his dick? What do you want from me?"

"Who is he? Who was his father, his mother—I want the story of his life, as much as you know of it."

"Why do you care?"

"Never mind," I said, "It's important to me. Just tell me; it can't hurt you to let me know."

She sat down on the ratty couch, and played with her long hair. I noticed she was bleary-eyed, maybe from alcohol. She seemed unusually dirty and ragged. Suddenly she struck me as more vulnerable than I had imagined. Maybe she cared, after all, although *what* she cared about, I wasn't sure; or could it be just the ordeal?

"Sophie, talk to me," I said.

"Alright, alright... since you're so damn interested. Not that I know very much."

"His family. Tell me about his family."

"He doesn't have a family. He doesn't even know who his father was. Maybe nobody knew. His mother... she was a loser, like him, only worse. A drug addict. Shoplifting, prostitution: I don't know. She probably had no idea who Tommy's father was. Not that it made any difference."

"What was her name?"

"I don't know. Mary something. She was a drifter. He was in and out of foster homes. Every once in a while she'd come back and take him, until she got so drunk or so high on cocaine or whatever it was, that the courts would take him away from her. Or she would just give him away. That's what Tommy's life was like: he was bounced around like a soccer ball. If I wasn't such a bitch, I'd feel sorry for him."

"And did he... get into trouble?"

"Tommy? Not much. A little. Stealing, stuff like that. Nothing major. Tommy is basically a wimp. A loser. He hasn't got the brains or the guts to do anything seriously bad."

"But, they have him on a murder charge. Two murders maybe. Maybe even three."

She laughed. "What a joke. Tommy never killed anybody. Never. I would bet any amount of money on that. But when the police get you and they make up their minds, you've had it: don't you know that? They've got some evidence against him, or they say they do, and if they need more, they'll make it up."

"You really believe that?"

"Mister, I *know* that. I don't trust cops. Why should I? They've got Tommy, and they'll never let him go. Besides, I told you, he's a loser. The only luck he ever had in his life, was Harriet Wingate. Now she's dead."

"And... Fosco?"

"I'm not saying anything about Fosco. I don't know who killed him, only it wasn't Tommy."

"But, the connection between them?"

"Fosco... Fosco and Tommy? Yeah... Fosco knew something. He knew Tommy in the past. That's all I'm going to say."

"They knew each other, Sophie? In what connection? Come on. I think you know. Tell me about it."

But she jumped up at that point, her face was grim, and I could see that she was shutting me down. "I've got to pack," she said, "I'm not talking anymore."

"Sophie."

"Go screw yourself," she said. And those were her final words.

21

I left Sophie's place feeling depressed. What she told me was tantalizing, but it wasn't enough. I needed more facts, and I wondered, would I ever get them?

But in fact the breakthrough came the very next day. I had gone out to lunch with a client, a young engineer, a boyish and eager man, armed with a recent degree from Stanford in Electrical Engineering. He wanted to discuss his great idea for a start-up company. In my experience, most start-up companies become end-up companies; I had no reason to think his company would be any different. I listened to his extremely clever idea for a new kind of software, and my eyes glazed over. His company was going to make a billion, he was sure. At least a billion. I suggested the names of some venture capitalists.

Honestly, I had no idea what his software could do or why it was a breakthrough, if it was. In the end I was the one who picked up the check for lunch. I could see myself working long hours trying to get his company in good legal order. And what would I have in the end? He could not, at this point, afford legal fees. He proposed giving me stock or stock options or the like.

Stock options are great when companies make money or they go public and everybody, including the people sweeping the floor, become millionaires. Otherwise they're nothing. I have a collection of those things already. I don't need any more. I long since gave up the idea of becoming stinking rich. I don't buy lottery tickets either.

When I walked back into the office, bored, tired, and frustrated, I was surprised to see Peter Elver sitting outside in the hallway waiting for me. He was pale, and his hands were shaking. He looked like death warmed over.

"Peter," I said, "What are you doing here?"

He said: "Frank, I have to talk to you. Do you have some time?"

"For you, Peter, sure. I don't have anybody coming in for at least an hour."

"Can we talk privately?"

"Of course," I said. I opened the door to my office. His eyes were bloodshot, and he looked like he hadn't shaved in days. Stubble, I know, is in, but not Peter's kind. I thought he had aged ten years since I saw him last.

I said, "Peter, you look terrible."

"Thanks. I feel terrible."

"Are you sick? Or is this some kind of trouble?"

He said, "It's more than trouble, Frank. It's the end of the line for me."

That sounded drastic. I motioned him to sit down. His hands were trembling worse than ever. He looked like somebody suffering from a particularly nasty kind of flu. He sat down on the chair; and I waited for him to start talking. He was clutching a dirty brown briefcase, scuffed and peeling. He bent his head over, and for a minute I couldn't see his face. He said nothing, and soon I saw why: he was sobbing convulsively. I felt helpless and, frankly, somewhat embarrassed. "Can I get you something?" I said, feebly. "Uh, coffee?"

"No, nothing.... I'll... get a grip on myself. I'm sorry I'm blubbering this way."

I waited. He calmed down a bit. I said, "What's the matter, Peter? Is it really that bad?"

"It couldn't be worse, Frank," he said between sobs. He wiped his eyes with a rather dirty-looking handkerchief. "Frank," he said, "I'm finished. I've ruined my life. It's all over for me. And it's all my fault. I've been a fool... no, I've been worse than a fool. I've been an idiot. An idiot. And I can't blame anybody... it was all me."

Then the words came tumbling out in a kind of mad rush. First, two failed marriages and support payment for rotten, ungrateful kids. Then an alcohol problem. Under control (he said). Then a gambling issue. And that one, that issue, well, it wasn't exactly under control.

I knew what was coming, as soon as I heard the words "trust funds." Here it was: the original sin of lawyers. He had gambled away the money that people gave him to manage. He had spent money that clients had left in trust naming him as trustee, and money in estates where he was executor. He had borrowed it, that's all. That's what he told himself: he was just borrowing it. (Of course, that's what they all say.) And he had gone to Vegas with the money, because he was already in debt and his only hope was to win big, win back the money, but no, he dug himself into a deeper and deeper hole....

It was an old story, I thought, a familiar story. No wonder he was so agitated. This was one absolutely sure way to get yourself disbarred: steal money from a client. Peter Elver's career would be over if this got out—and I assumed it *was* getting out, that's why he was such a total wreck. People are such fools. Do they really think nobody will ever find out? Do people who run Ponzi schemes think they can carry on forever?

But why was he telling me these things? Where did I come in?

I listened and tried to be as supportive as I could. I made sympathetic clucking noises. I even put my hand on his shoulder. Actually, I didn't feel the least bit of sympathy, but I put on a decent show. I am not sure why I put on this show. It's hard to do otherwise, when somebody is blubbering right in front of you, even a thief.

"It's bad, Peter," I said, "I know that. But you're not the first... or the last. I mean, to take money that belongs to the clients. It's big trouble, I know that; but maybe they'll give you a break. The disciplinary committee, I mean. Maybe just a suspension, Peter. Maybe it's not the end of the world."

"I know that... but, Frank, you haven't heard the worst."

"The worst?"

"It's not just that I lost the money: that would be bad enough. But I owed more, lots more, big money... I spent *all* my money, *all* this clients' money, and then I just ran up more debts... I fell into the hands of gangsters, loan sharks...."

I began to sense what was coming. He went on, telling it all, spilling his guts, and then I heard a magic name. "...this guy, this mobster, Vincent Fosco...."

"Did you say Vincent Fosco?" I asked. Of course, I knew he had said it. "The one whose body they found? The one they said Tommy Wingate killed?"

"That's the one. Fosco. He was horrible, Frank. A thug. The worst of the worst. And violent.... I was scared, frightened to death of him. He was vicious, a killer, I heard he had killed guys! I couldn't pay him, and he had me by the balls; what could I do?"

"I don't know, Peter. What *could* you do?"

"He had a scheme to get money, a blackmail scheme. He wanted my help. He was blackmailing this woman...."

It clicked in my brain. "Harriet Wingate."

"Yes. Harriet Wingate. How did you guess? Yes, she was paying him money—not directly though, he was too clever for that. I set up a dummy company, I called it the Anguilla Corporation, I opened an account, and she paid the money into this account. Every month. I was trustee of the account. And I transferred the money to Fosco."

"But, Peter, what was this all about? Blackmail? Harriet Wingate? A rich old lady? What could he possibly have on her?"

"At the time I didn't know. I didn't really care, either. I only knew it was something to do with that young guy, Tommy. I told you, I didn't know, and I didn't care. All I wanted was to get out from under, get Fosco off my back; and maybe make enough money to keep from getting exposed, getting disbarred... maybe pay some of the trust money back...."

Something came to me in a flash. It wasn't a stroke of genius. But here, finally, was somebody with a real, genuine honest-to-God motive for killing Vincent Fosco. "Peter, I've got to ask you this, straight out. Did you *kill* this guy Fosco?"

"Frank, look at me: could I kill anybody, even a gangster like that? Never in a million years. I'm a weakling! I have no guts, maybe that's my whole problem. Look, I didn't even know he was dead. I swear it. He just disappeared on me, I had no idea where he went, and what happened to him. One day he was there, the next day he wasn't. After a few weeks, I kind of breathed a sigh of relief: the guy was gone. I didn't know where he went, and I didn't care. I only hoped it was far, far away."

I thought of Fosco's body, buried in the woods, with coyotes or whatever nibbling at his flesh and bones. Fosco had indeed gone about as far away as anybody could possibly go. "You're sure you didn't know he was dead?"

"Absolutely; Frank, look, I'm spilling my guts out to you, I'm debasing myself: why would I lie?"

"OK. Still, he was gone. You were off the hook, Peter. I mean, when Fosco disappeared."

"Yes and no, Frank. I couldn't be sure. Fosco could come back, any minute and I'd be in the soup again. And I still needed money, big money. I had to have money, to make good the money I took from that trust. So I turned to blackmail myself, I continued the scheme, I squeezed money out of Mrs. Wingate...."

"Peter, that's disgusting. I have to say it. How could you?"

"Don't judge me, Frank. You think I'm disgusting? What do you think I think about myself? But yes. I did it. I blackmailed Harriet Wingate."

"But how, Peter? You didn't even know what it was all about. That's what you just told me."

"I know it, so I had to lie. I told her I was, well, the agent for Fosco's partners. I didn't want to say I represented Fosco himself: I was afraid he would come back and.... Anyway, I told her there was a syndicate. Fosco, I said, was just one of the low-level people, a thug, nobody important in the organization; and I represented the big guys, I was their agent. And the syndicate wanted more money. I think she suspected I was telling a bunch of lies. But how could she be sure? At first I asked for $3,000 a month, then I upped the ante, eventually I made it $6,000 a month. She paid. And paid and paid. No questions asked. After all, she was a very rich woman."

"And then what happened?"

"Frank, believe me: this is painful for me. You can't know... how ashamed I am of what I did. But I was desperate. Truly desperate. I needed the money so that I could cover up the losses, at least for a while. I thought the money doesn't matter to her; she's old, she can't live long. Somebody told me she was sick: cancer or something. Now I know that wasn't true. Still, she did die, didn't she? Anyway, I was getting money, and I had a scheme, for more money...."

"A scheme, Peter? What sort of scheme?"

"Well, it involved a young woman...."

"Let me guess: her name is Sophie."

"You know about her? It doesn't surprise me.... She had some kind of connection to Vincent Fosco, I guess. Maybe she was his niece. I don't know. Anyway, before he disappeared, she came on the scene. And, well, this was the scheme, I think Fosco had something to do with it: she got her hooks into this young guy, Tommy. It wasn't particularly hard to do. She's attractive and available.... They got an apartment together."

"And what *was* the scheme?"

"In a way, it was perfectly legal. She just wanted Harriet Wingate's money, and she thought she was going to get it through Tommy, because he would inherit the money. Not all of it, but part of it, and Harriet Wingate was filthy rich. His share would be millions."

"Why was she so sure he was going to get the money? Was it because Tommy was married to Harriet Wingate?"

"I mean, wasn't that weird? To this day, I can't understand it... how the two of them got married. Not that there was any sex or anything like that! Look: I mean, he was living with Sophie. Weird. But Sophie, she knew, marriage or no marriage, there would be bushels of money. Harriet had some kind of thing for this Tommy. He was like a son to her, or a grandson, or something. There was a rumor that he *was* her grandson, but I don't believe that. If he was, why would she marry him? Anyway, Sophie knew that the old lady was going to leave half of her fortune to the guy, or maybe she just figured it out. So she, Sophie, was bound and determined to get her hands on that money. And I'd get my share."

"A nice pair, you two."

"Frank, I don't need that. Give me a break. Well, she didn't get the money... not yet... and maybe she never will. But she got Tommy: that was the easy part. They moved in together, and he moved out of Harriet's house."

"And that was *before* this, uh, marriage? Is that what you said?"

"I'm pretty sure it was. Maybe. I don't know for sure. Anyway, Harriet didn't take to Sophie. She was a shrewd old woman, very smart—well, you knew her—and there was something about Sophie that she didn't like. I think she guessed what the game was. After all, it wasn't as if Sophie was exactly Tommy's type. Or maybe I mean vice versa."

"How so?"

"Well... I never met Tommy, but he was pretty much a dim-wit; that's what Sophie said anyway, and Sophie was nobody's fool. Sophie knew what she wanted, and she was willing to put up with Tommy. Harriet probably saw right through it. And what's more, I think she suspected that there was some connection between Sophie and me, and the whole Vincent Fosco business. She definitely smelled a rat."

"How do you know all this?"

"Sophie talked to me. And then, well, there was the whole business with that will...."

"The cat will?"

"Exactly. Harriet came to me, and I was, of course, surprised: she wasn't my client. I was suspicious immediately. She said she wanted to make out a will. She was asking a guy who blackmailed her, to be her lawyer! That was pretty weird. But I said sure, of course, I do that sort of work. Then she proceeded to give me instructions about the will, this business of leaving everything to cats."

"You believed her?"

"I did and I didn't. I got the message. She was saying not a penny to Tommy, she was saying the game is up, I see through you and Sophie. It was a warning. Look: I didn't know she was allergic to cats. I actually thought this was on the up-

and-up. She's telling me it's all going to charity, you and that woman are wasting your time...."

He stopped, and mopped his forehead. He was under a terrific strain, that was obvious. And where was this going? Was this some sort of confession? But he already said he hadn't killed Vincent Fosco.

22

I stared at Peter. A lot of things were becoming clear. Not all, but Peter's statement cleared up some of the mysteries. I pressed on:

"You told me some friend of Harriet's referred her to you, that you didn't really know her and all that," I said.

"Those were lies."

"OK. Go on," I said.

"Well, things seemed to be falling apart.... I was getting more and more nervous. Then I heard about Vincent Fosco, that they found the body.... I was in a way relieved. I was rid of him forever, but then I started to wonder, who killed him? Of course I figured it could be anybody—a gangster like that, they kill each other all the time. But I was nervous. I felt the whole scheme was unraveling somehow. And then there was Sophie: she was getting nervous too. She said she was going to split, she didn't want to stick around anymore unless she could be sure she'd be getting the money, and fairly soon.

"So we talked things over, me and Sophie. The wills, that sort of thing. I said I thought it was just a smoke screen, I said I thought the cat will was a fake, that Harriet Wingate tore it up as soon as she got home, and that she *was* going to leave her money to Tommy. But Sophie said, how can we be sure? Well, we didn't know. So... well, things were just hanging, and we didn't know where they were heading. Then one night Sophie called me. She said Harriet was going to be away, out of town the next day, and the house was going to be empty. We could go into the house and find out...."

"Who? *You?*"

"Well, she said *she* might go, if she could get away from Tommy. Otherwise, I should go. There was no danger she said, nobody was home.... Of course, the old lady had lied, she never went away, she *was* home that night, the night she died. But we didn't know what. Anyway, Sophie gave me a key and told me where to look for the will, she told me where the old lady kept things. She gave me the burglar alarm code, too. She said everything would be perfectly safe, the whole business. She said she'd call me if she went...."

"She did go."

"Yes, *now* I know that, but I didn't then. She should have called me before she went, but she just wasn't thinking straight. She went there, and of course the big surprise was that Harriet *was* home that night.... Sophie got out of there in a real hurry, and *then* she called me. She left a message on my voicemail, but I was already out of the house. I thought Sophie hadn't gone after all; I figured she'd have called by the time I left home."

"What time was this?"

"I don't remember. Nine. Ten. Maybe later, something. Anyway, I thought now I have to do it myself. I was scared, but I felt it had to be done, so I went. I went to Harriet Wingate's house, drove there, parked...."

"Wait a minute: when you came to see me about the wills, you said you were out of town when she died, that you didn't come back for a while, that you didn't even know she was dead."

"Frank: what can I say? Those were lies. I did leave town, but afterwards...."

"OK, go on."

"Alright: there I was, at the Wingate house...."

"And?"

"I didn't know Sophie had been there. And I certainly didn't know the old lady was home. It was completely dark. I let myself in with the key. Funny thing, the burglar alarm was off, I didn't need to turn it off. Anyway, I turned on a night light in a downstairs bathroom and I had a pocket flashlight with me. I went upstairs and I started searching for the will. I went into Mrs. Wingate's room. I started looking in the drawer of the dresser, and then, I don't know how, but suddenly, I became aware that she was *there.*"

"She made a noise."

"God, no. She wasn't making any noise. She was dead, Frank. Well, I didn't know that at the time. But, I guess the light from the flashlight.... I could tell there was somebody in the bed, and I thought, oh God, she's here, what'll I do? But she seemed to be in a deep sleep, and then, I don't know what it was, some kind of intuition, but somehow I knew something was wrong. I went over to the bed. She looked... funny. I knew she was dead. Don't ask me how, I just knew it. I felt panicky. I tried her pulse: nothing. I thought, oh my God, the old lady died on me, and here I am! But what was she doing there? Sophie had told me she'd be out of town! I can't tell you what I felt, the panic, the horror...."

"What did you do?"

"I couldn't think. I was sweating, I was totally beside myself. Frank, you can imagine: a dead body. Well, if I had been rational, I would have realized she's dead, she can't hurt me, she can't call out. But it just got to me: I was totally rattled. I just stood there for a while. Shivering. Then I pulled myself together. I said Peter, you came to get something, go get it. So I calmed myself, and I started looking again. There was a folder on the end table next to the old lady's bed. A bright yellow manila folder. You know the kind. Inside of it was an envelope, a thick envelope. It wasn't sealed, and I opened it, thinking it might just possibly be the will...."

"And was it?"

"No. It was a long letter addressed to Barbara, I think; but it wasn't a will. I didn't read it, I didn't have time. I put it back inside the envelope, then I went over to the dresser, and then I went into the study, and I used my flashlight, and I kept on looking for the will."

"And?"

"And I found it."

"You found it?"

"It was there. The will. Her last will. I read it over quickly, and I stuffed it in my pocket. I've still got it."

"Good God, Peter... you *stole* it, Harriet Wingate's will?"

"I know, I know. I know it's a crime. But it's only one more thing. I was already in so deep, I had done so many stupid things, this was only one thing more."

"But what did the will say? It wasn't the cat will, was it?"

"No, of course not. No, it was a regular will. I only glanced at it to get the gist of it. Then I took it with me; later on I read it at my place. Nothing special. It left some money to friends, a few small gifts to charity, and there was a nice bit of money to somebody named Joe Pangea. I don't know who he is, but she left him money. The rest was divided, one half to Tommy, the other half to Barbara and Karen."

"But this is what Sophie wanted," I said. "She wanted you to get that will. That was the whole point. The scheme worked, right? Tommy was going to get half of the estate, that's millions for him, and for Sophie, if she kept her hooks on him. You... you told Sophie about the will, didn't you? Why didn't you offer it to probate?"

"Frank, you've got to understand me.... No, I didn't tell Sophie about the will. I wanted something to... use against her. After all, how could I get a share of the money, Tommy's money? She could just tell me to go to hell, to shut up or she'd talk to the bar association! I mean, she *knew* about me. Look: I know I was doing one stupid thing after another. I couldn't admit I had the will. How did I get it? Once I took it... I did want the will probated, only I didn't know *how* to do it. So I delayed, one day after another, and I just held on to it until now."

This was amazing. I leaned back and let it sink in. I had had a suspicion about Peter: something about the whole cat will just wasn't kosher. But until now I had no clue as to what was going on. No question, he had cleared up a lot of things. But not everything, of course. "So, Peter, let me get this straight: when you came to me about the cat will, that was just play-acting."

"I'm sorry, Frank. Basically, yes. I knew she had probably torn up that will. But I just had to know whether there was yet another will, and what the situation was. I knew the will I had in my hands was the last one: it was dated the day she died, after all. As far as the cat will is concerned, I had a copy of that one, so I came to you with that. But, generally speaking, I was just reconnoitering."

A lot of light bulbs were flashing all over the place. One in particular. "Peter," I said, "that folder, the one by the bed: tell me more about it."

"I told you everything I know."

"Tell me again."

"There's nothing to tell. There was this yellow folder by the bed. I looked inside, I told you, there was some sort of letter, I didn't read it, I just put it back in the folder. That's all."

"But... there was no folder there, by the bed, when Barbara and I looked for the will. I'm positive of that. What happened to it? The cleaning lady found Harriet dead the next morning. Did she take it? I can't imagine she would. Barbara and I came over the next day, I think. It was before the funeral, I remember that. We looked and looked; we were looking for the will. There was nothing there at all. You're sure: a folder, and a long letter inside?"

"Positive. Does it matter?"

"Not to you, Peter, to be blunt about it; but it may matter a very great deal to other people," I said. "So the question is: where is that folder now?"

"I don't know."

"Somebody took that folder," I said.

"Not me. I swear it."

"Are you sure, Peter?"

"Frank, I've told you so many terrible things, why would I lie about that stupid folder?"

Why indeed. I had to believe him. Things were wildly racing around in my mind. I had to think. Who could have taken that folder? Who had access to the house? Lots of people: Tommy, Sophie. But that didn't make much sense. There was somebody else.

Then I remembered who. Of course. But, could it possibly be?

For what earthly reason? My mind was whirling around like leaves in a storm....

Peter, of course, couldn't care less about the folder. He was interested only in his own miserable self. He was sitting there sobbing again, wallowing in his unhappiness, blubbering about the way he had ruined his life. I tried to be supportive, but it was hard for me. Between the sobs, he told me that he was going to the police, or maybe he said he had gone to the police, and he was going to give me the will, or give them the will. Anyway, he was going to tell them about everything, he couldn't go on, he was ready to take his medicine, and so on.

"The toughest thing," he said between sobs, "is how I'm going to face Sandra."

I had no idea who Sandra was, and really didn't care. Sandra turned out to be his daughter, who lived in Dayton, and had very little use for him anyway ever since his divorce. I couldn't wait to get him out of the office so I could pursue my hunch about that folder.

"Do you think they'll disbar me?" he asked at the door.

It was pitiful. His eyes were still full of tears. I muttered something about remorse: I told him if he promised to make restitution, sometimes they are pretty lenient, that he should be hopeful, that sort of thing. In my humble opinion he was a 100% certain candidate for disbarment, considering all the things he had done, but now was not the time to break the news to him.

He finally left after more crying, soul-searching, and pitiful appeals for sympathy. I gripped him on the shoulder and squeezed him. I tried to look like a friend. I made sure he left me the will. That's what I cared most about. That and the yellow folder. Peter of course was in a pathetic state of disarray. Despite my soothing words, I had very little sympathy for him. He was, frankly, despicable; his stupid actions had caused no end of trouble; and he deserved whatever he was going to get. But I put on a show as best I could.

23

I breathed a sigh of relief when Peter was gone. I couldn't wait to get on the phone.

I dialed a familiar number. I crossed my fingers. Please, let her be home! Please, Lord, no voicemail.

I was in luck. Karen was in fact at home.

"Karen, it's Frank," I said. "I have good news and bad news."

"OK, I'll bite. What's the good news?"

"The good news is that I have the real will. The actual will. Your aunt's last will and testament. Made out shortly before she died. It gives some small gifts to friends, charity, and a bit more to Joe Pangea. It names Barbara as executor, you and Barbara get half, Tommy gets half; it's all legal and proper. It's not the will I drew up—I'm sure she destroyed that will. But it's a real, genuine will."

"Where did you get it?"

"It's a long story, Karen. I'll tell it to you some time, but not now. Now the bad news."

"What's that?"

"I know what you did. I know that you took the yellow folder."

There was a pause, then she said, "Frank, don't be mysterious. What folder?"

"The folder by your aunt's bed, Karen. There was a folder there with a long letter inside, the night she died. A bright yellow folder. Unmistakable. And inside was an envelope, and inside the envelope was a letter. You took it, Karen."

"I don't know what you're talking about."

"Karen, it's me, Frank," I said. "It's not the police, it's me: I'm your attorney. Please don't lie to me. Anyway, I know all about the folder."

Silence.

"Karen, I *know* you took that folder. It was gone when Barbara and I came to the house. Nobody else was even around at the time. Edna found the body, and she called you on the phone. You came right over. I'm sure it was there, right there, by the bed. You must have seen it. You went up to look at the body, and you must have taken it. Who else could it be? For sure it wasn't Edna. It had to be you."

More silence.

"Karen, I know there was a letter inside that folder. I'd like to know what the letter said. It's important. Please, you've got to confide in me."

You could cut the silence with a knife. I said, "Are you there?"

She was there. I was afraid she had hung up on me, but she hadn't. She was obviously thinking. "I'm waiting, Karen," I said, trying to sound gentle but firm.

Finally, she spoke: "It *is* important," she said. "You don't know how important... Frank," she added. "I've been bad. I've... done something terribly wrong."

"That's obvious."

"I... made a big mistake."

"We all make mistakes, Karen."

"Can I come see you? I don't want to talk about it over the phone."

"OK," I said, "you'd better come over."

She promised that she would: "I'll be there as soon as I can." I had a feeling—which turned out to be true—that the last of the pieces were about to fall into place.

I was on pins and needles waiting for Karen. I had a client in the office, and I hope she couldn't tell how distracted I was. She was a middle-aged woman, divorced, unhappy about the way her only daughter treated her. We were discussing what kind of will she should make out, whether to leave a lot to the daughter or very little, and so on. "Frank," she said, "she's my only child, my flesh and blood. She treats me like... oh, I can't describe it. Why should *she* get my hard-earned money? And yet, I love her and there's nobody else...."

I thought she would never go.

I'm glad Celia wasn't around to see what I was doing: she would disapprove of my attitude. She doesn't like it when I act as if I'm an amateur detective. Not that I really *am* an amateur detective. I don't think I could solve my way out of a paper bag. But sometimes, as I said, well, it more or less falls in my lap.

Karen appeared, sort of breathless and a little bit disheveled (or perhaps I was imagining that). She was obviously somewhat agitated. I offered her some coffee, which she refused. She sat down in front of me, played with her purse, and suddenly started to cry.

I offered her a Kleenex, which she took eagerly.

"I didn't mean any harm," she said.

"I know," I said. Of course I knew nothing of the sort.

"I was trying to... protect the family," she said.

"Sure. Of course, Karen."

"How do you know about the letter?"

"It's a long story, Karen. Believe it or not, somebody was in the house that night, actually two people. . It was downright crowded in there. One of them saw the folder, and told me about it."

"Oh God."

"And... since it wasn't there when we looked for it, I started thinking, who could have taken it? And you were the obvious person."

Sobs. I handed her another Kleenex.

"You say somebody saw it. Who was that, Frank?"

"I'd rather not say."

She seemed to accept that. She nodded her head yes. She was silent for a while, absorbed in her sobbing.

First Peter, then Karen. That was a lot of sobbing for a lawyer's office. Of course, they weren't the first, and no doubt they wouldn't be the last. But I prefer clients who don't sob, and have no reason to sob.

Finally Karen dabbed at her eyes with the tissue, cleared

her throat, and began to talk. She said, "I guess you can't get away with anything in this life. Or maybe it's just that *I* can't. But... I thought it was harmless, really. When I picked up the folder... it was open, you know. I started reading it and I saw immediately, it was a suicide note. But then there were other things in it. Terrible things, Frank, simply terrible things. I was. aghast. I didn't know what to do...."

"When was this, Karen?"

"The morning after... after Aunt Harriet died. Edna called me. You know that. I came over, and I went up to the room. I saw the folder. Edna was in the next room by then. The ambulance came... it was a horrible scene, as you can imagine. I was upset, of course, about Aunt Harriet, and the letter, that was even *more* upsetting. I had one of those really big purses, and I slipped the folder into it. I didn't really finish reading it until I got home."

"Do you still have it, Karen?"

"I do," she said. "I have it right here with me."

"But why did you do this, Karen? What were you thinking?"

"The shame, Frank. I have a lot of family pride. You know how much family means to me. I'm a Spively. I'm proud of my heritage! I thought, here's my aunt, she's a Spively too, she has the same heritage. Here she is, confessing such awful things, and then she takes her own life. I just was overwhelmed with shame."

"Karen, can you back up a little. *What* awful things was she confessing?"

"You don't know, Frank?"

"No, I really don't."

She hesitated for a minute. "Well, I might as well tell you. I can't keep this a secret, not anymore. I'm going to go to the police with it. I feel so... guilty. Can you help me think up a story, Frank, something to explain why I waited so long?"

"Why not tell them the truth?" I asked. She nodded her head, and began sobbing again. It was time for another tissue.

She blew her nose and wiped her eyes. "You're right, Frank. I should have talked to you before. But the truth is so painful! I can't tell you how painful. The truth is my aunt confessed to murder. She says so, right here: she killed this man Vincent Fosco. She shot him! And now she was killing herself! Can you imagine how I felt when I read that? I had no idea who Vincent Fosco was. Now I know. But maybe *you* should read it, Frank. I was so shocked. Imagine, a Spively. And my own aunt... And then I thought, who's to know? And why *should* they know? I couldn't see any reason. And, as far as the suicide is concerned, why not let them think she died a natural death. An old lady, dead in her bed, no marks on her, no signs: nobody would know. There wouldn't be any investigation, no autopsy, or anything like that. Just let her lie in peace. So I kept quiet, Frank. Do you think I'm a terrible person?"

"Oh, no, Karen; not at all," I said. What else could I say? "You acted from the highest of motives."

"Oh, I did, I did. And it's been awful for me, these last few days. Ever since they arrested Tommy. That was the final blow. I can't let him rot in prison, Frank. I can't let them try him for murder. Maybe Barbara would do that: she's capable of it, she hates him so. But believe me, I couldn't do it. I just couldn't."

I agreed, nodding my head. She went on: "I should have done this right away. As soon as I heard that they'd arrested him. But I was so frightened. I was hoping they'd let him go, and then it would be all right. And then when they didn't... I knew I had to *do* something, but I didn't know what. I'm a coward, Frank. I should have gone right away. The poor boy, in jail...."

I said, "Why don't you show me the letter?"

She reached into her purse and pulled it out. "This is the original. I made a copy, too. I went to a FedEx place in the middle of the night. I didn't want anybody to see me."

The saga of the trip to the copy place didn't interest me. I took the letter from her hands. It was a long document, many pages, written in a beautiful hand, a small, delicate hand, the hand of an old woman who learned penmanship when she was young, the way they used to teach it. I sat there and read every word. It was an amazing story. I won't quote it directly, but I'll paraphrase for you what it said.

24

The letter was, in the first instance, a suicide note. She said she had lived a long, full life, and was ready to die. She would have preferred to go on living: she was healthy and she had a lot to live for. But under the circumstances she had no choice. She said the letter would explain it all—explain why she decided it was time to go.

It then backtracked and began telling the story of her life. How she was pretty wild as a young woman, very wild, in fact, for those days. She was the despair of her parents. They were respectable people, strait-laced in fact, churchgoers, very concerned with what the neighbors would think. They came from an old family and were very proud of their heritage, proud of their position in society. And she was *not* what they expected from a proper young woman: she was out of control. She ran around with what they used to call a "bad crowd." Then, at age 18 or so, she found herself "in trouble." Pregnant, in short. The father was some man she met at a dance, a married man. He wanted nothing to do with her and refused to take any responsibility. His name doesn't matter now, said the letter; he had died many years ago.

Her parents were horrified, of course. And selfish, she said. All they cared about was avoiding scandal: *her* feelings didn't seem to matter to them. They whisked her out of town and she gave birth to a child in Phoenix, a baby boy. She never saw the child, not really.. He was given up for adoption, privately, on the spot. She thinks money changed hands, but she doesn't know. In later years, she often thought about the baby, but she never tried to trace her son. The whole thing had been totally hushed up. Nobody knew about it outside of her parents and one or two close friends of the family. Her parents would have died if this scandal had become general knowledge.

Then someone introduced her to Joseph Wingate. He liked her, he courted her, and they got married. He was twenty years older than she was. He was a good man and it was a good match, everybody said. She didn't really love him, she had to admit, but she respected him. He loved her, and was kind to her. Before they got married, she had told him about her past, about the baby. He didn't care, he said, but it was clear he didn't want her to find her child, or even to think about it. It was a closed book as far as he was concerned.

Her marriage was good, she had no regrets on that score. But they never had any children. They were married about nineteen years, and then he died. He had become diabetic and he had heart trouble; and a heart attack ended his life. He had been rich when she met him, and he got richer during the marriage. He left her everything, a fortune She had guarded the fortune carefully, investing shrewdly and living modestly. By now she had a very considerable amount of money.

But when he died, she felt quite alone. Yes, she had two wonderful nieces who lived nearby; they were kind and attentive, almost like daughters to her. But she felt... an emptiness. At this point in her life, she became obsessed with the idea of finding her son. She hired detectives. Everything was hush-hush: she never told her nieces, or anybody else.

And she did get, eventually, a report about her son, a report that shocked and depressed her. He had turned out very badly. He grew up twisted and evil, a violent, dangerous man. He was in trouble as a juvenile, and then, as an adult, amassed a long criminal record. You can imagine how she felt. She was overcome with guilt. She wondered... if she had *kept* him, if she had raised him, loved him, cared for him, would he have turned out differently?

Then she made a serious mistake. Though she never actually met him, she did communicate with him. She might have known that no good would come of it. He had no interest in his mother, but her money was another matter. He wanted cash for lawyers, to pay off debts, to get him out of trouble. At first, she gave him some money. But nothing changed in his life. He wanted more and more. She refused. She told him never to get in touch with her again.

And then came the incident that cost him his life: the terrible crime he committed, and the way he paid for it. Maybe she could have avoided this tragedy, too. Maybe if she had given him the money he wanted, things would have turned out differently. Rationally, she knew this wasn't the case, but the thought only added to her guilt. She was getting old, she was alone, and she had this terrible secret she couldn't share with anybody.

Her son committed the worst crime of his life: he kidnapped and murdered a whole family. I remembered the newspaper clippings she had kept in her drawer. They were about her son. This time he didn't get away with his crime, of course, and he ended up dead. She knew from the newspapers that he hadn't been alone at the time he killed those people. There was another man with him, and a woman, and a boy of sixteen. The woman and the child intrigued her. She hired detectives again, to find *them*, find out who they were and what their story was. The search was difficult. They were fugitives from justice. The police couldn't find them, so how could she? But her detectives persisted, she poured money into the search, and in the end, she was successful.

What she found out was roughly this: the woman and the boy were innocent victims of her son. The woman was a pathetic creature, a drug addict, a former prostitute, a thief. Harriet's son had moved in with her, dominated her, taken advantage of her. The boy was her child by some unknown father. He had spent much of his life shuttled from foster home to foster home. In between foster homes, his mother would kick her habit for a while, experience a spasm of guilt, and take him back, only to lose him during her next bout of drunkenness or drug-based madness. And her latest man, Harriet's son, cared nothing for the boy: he was a brutal, uncaring stepfather.

The boy's name was Tommy.

Shortly before Harriet found him, Tommy's mother had finally died of an overdose. And Tommy? He had been living on the streets, then sometimes in juvenile shelters. Now she had one clear, clean object to concentrate on: the boy. Tommy was a young man now, a lost soul, the latest victim of her dead son, *her* latest victim. She, after all, had set in motion a dreadful cycle of events, which ended up this way. This boy had nobody, he was alone, living like a hunted animal. His life had been sacrificed on the altar of her youthful mistakes.

Harriet took an awful chance: Tommy could have been a ruined soul, a young thug, somebody brutalized by life and beyond redemption. But she had to try. She brought Tommy back to her house. She gave him odd jobs to do and a room to sleep in. She tried to bring order and love into his life. And he responded. Somehow, in all the turmoil of his life, he had never learned to be vicious and antisocial. He was weak, bewildered, defeated. But there was nothing evil about him, and he reacted to her kindness with dogged, tenacious love. She and Tommy became close friends. He became... like one of the family: he even started using her last name. She wanted that. His own name meant nothing to him. He took some classes at night, he tried hard. He was hardly a natural student. But eventually he earned a high school diploma.

All this made her very happy. In some small way, she was making amends. But it was too good to be true, too good to last. It came to a bitter end. Vincent Fosco appeared on the scene. Harriet was the answer to Fosco's prayers: a golden goose, a rich and abundant source of money. He began to blackmail her. What was the threat? He could turn Tommy over to the police; they still believed, Fosco said, that Tommy was part of the murder plot. Of course, Fosco had been an accomplice himself, if not worse: he himself was at risk. But he gambled, correctly, that Harriet would never betray him for fear that Tommy too would be betrayed.

She paid and paid. She dealt only with Fosco. As far as she knew, Fosco was acting on his own. She was willing to pay, she had no choice. But Fosco was insatiable. He kept raising the ante; the more she paid, the more he wanted. The money wasn't really the issue—she had plenty of money, but she found it more and more painful to live with this shadow on their lives. Tommy too was terrifically upset. And Fosco... he would appear from time to time at the house, sometimes drunk, sometimes abusive. They had a terrible scene one day. Tommy was out at the time. Fosco was drunk or high on drugs, and he became enraged and beat her badly. When Tommy came home, they had to call the doctor.

The situation became intolerable. She thought about killing Fosco. But she didn't want to reveal this plan to Tommy. She didn't want him to be involved in any way. God forbid! Above all, she wanted him never again to be entangled in somebody else's crime. But then Fosco appeared again, drunk, abusive, threatening.

Tommy was upstairs in his room. She ordered him not to come down. She had gotten a pistol and she learned how to use it. She threatened Fosco. He laughed at her. He said she wouldn't dare. She shot him on the spot, firing the gun repeatedly. Fosco was mortally wounded. Tommy came down the stairs and stood there, horrified, as Fosco died in front of his eyes.

Now they were really in trouble. She tried to stay calm. She had wanted to spare Tommy, keep him from becoming involved; but now this was impossible. She had to have his help, who else could she turn to? After dark, they wrapped the body in a blanket, and put it in the car. They waited until late at night, then drove to a place in the woods, in the foothills, as remote a spot as they could find. Tommy dug a hole in the ground off the road, and they buried the body. They covered the spot with leaves, and they hoped it would never come to light. As she realized later, they made some ignorant mistakes. After all, they were rank amateurs. They knew they had to get rid of the gun. Tommy tied his jacket around it, and they buried it with the body. That was absolute stupidity, but she supposed they just weren't thinking clearly at the time.

She thought, though, that now they were safe. She thought the crisis was over—at least for the time being. She had no regrets about Fosco. He was a worm, a thug, a murderer, and he didn't deserve to live. She was not worried about herself—who would suspect an old woman of murder, or prosecute her for this crime? Old women were never criminals. She felt she was safe. In any event, who knows how long she had to live? But she worried about Tommy's situation. She worried about what might happen if somebody discovered the body. What if the finger of suspicion pointed at him, *or* her? How could they protect themselves? That's when she hit on the idea of getting married.

Tommy of course thought it was crazy. But she explained to him that husbands and wives couldn't testify against each other. The law had to leave them alone. That way, they would both be safe if trouble ever arose. (In fact, Harriet Wingate was a bit shaky on the exact state of the law, but then that's normal for lay people. The important point is what she *believed* to be the law.) She said she wanted Tommy to have part of her estate anyway, and this would make it easier. They got in the car and drove to Nevada, and they got married there. Naturally the minister thought it was a very peculiar marriage. But maybe it wasn't the first one he'd seen: a rich old lady, infatuated with some young gigolo? Why not? The minister said nothing, took their money, and performed the ceremony. Things went along as before for a while. Tommy had gotten together with Sophie, and he moved into Sophie's apartment. She, Harriet, paid the rent. Oh, she knew people would think the arrangement was very odd, since Tommy was legally her husband. But she didn't much care what they thought. She never liked Sophie, but did not want to interfere at first. As time went on, she began to get suspicious of Sophie's motives. And more and more she was convinced there was something wrong, that there was something or somebody behind Sophie, and that Tommy was the target.

Then the trouble began again: more blackmail. This time it came from a local lawyer named Peter Elver. He claimed to represent some of Fosco's associates. Harriet never quite believed him—there was a certain trumped-up quality about the story. Was he acting entirely on his own? She couldn't be sure.

It was a dangerous situation. She paid Elver what he asked for. But she felt trapped. Fosco was dead, and yet there seemed to be some sort of conspiracy, and she didn't know who or what was behind it. Her suspicions increased when by accident she saw Peter Elver and Sophie together in a restaurant, deep in conversation.

Harriet was a woman who believed in taking action. She decided to do something about Sophie and Peter Elver: this was what lay behind the "cat will." The will was, of course, a hoax. And, as I always suspected, it was some sort of message. It was directed to Peter Elver and was meant, among other things, to disabuse him of the idea that Sophie would get any money out of Tommy. And it gave her an excuse to visit Elver, to size him up, to try to decide if he was bluffing or not. But at the end of the session she was still somewhat unsure. Did he represent some sort of criminal syndicate? Were there more Vincent Fosco's out there in the world? She felt threatened, and she felt that Tommy was threatened too. These were, or might be, violent, unscrupulous men who would milk her of untold amounts of money, and who could ruin everything she had planned for Tommy's future.

Then came the discovery of Vincent Fosco's body. That was a serious blow: her own plot began to unravel. The police came around and questioned her. They started sniffing around Tommy. Harriet saw how foolish they had been. Even though a year had gone by, they had left too many clues behind: the gun, the jacket. Naturally, suspicion fell on Tommy, not on her. They were able somehow to identify the jacket, and the gun was traced to her household. Of course soon they also discovered Tommy's real identity, his past, and his role in the earlier murders. They convinced themselves that Tommy was a young punk who had killed Fosco after some kind of gangster quarrel, and probably had a hand in the Arizona murders, as an accomplice if nothing else.

She knew, in other words, that the game was up. And she was willing to accept this. She had tossed the dice and lost. There was only one way out. She made her plans carefully. She prepared a full confession: it was the document I was reading. She put her affairs in order. She gave Tommy a copy of a holographic will, a short version of what she wanted done with her money, in case something happened to the genuine will. She felt the time had come. She was afraid—of Peter Elver, of Sophie, of the unknown gangsters who may or may not have been lurking in the background. But she had to save Tommy from disaster. Her money could make him a secure and comfortable future. A surprise came into her life. She discovered she had a blood grandson, Joe Pangea. He seemed like a fine, upstanding young man. She prepared a new will. It was, in essence, the same as the old one, except that it left some money to Joe Pangea. She told nobody about him, for fear that he too would be drawn into the mess she had made of her affairs.

She made plans to end her own life. But she did have a desperate longing to meet her grandson and to see him at least once before she died. She told him to come down and visit her. And she warned Tommy about Sophie again. She went to their place the night before, and spoke to him bluntly. Tommy was weak and easily dominated, but he had always done what she wanted. She was sure he would listen to her. She made him promise he would break off the relationship. It might take him some time, but after she was gone, she knew he would do what she said, especially when he realized it was her dying wish.

She prepared everything carefully. She told her nieces she was going out of town. She told Tommy the same thing. She wanted nobody to come over that evening, except, of course, Joe Pangea. Then, after his visit, she would do the final deed. Did she want to die? Not really. But she had lived a long life, and to her way of thinking, suicide was the best solution to her troubles, and to Tommy's as well. After her death, he would have plenty of money, enough to defend himself against anything that might come up. Her confession should free him from suspicion. She was convinced the police would believe her story. She was proving it by taking her own life. They would realize how serious she was. They were bound to let Tommy go.

She was writing these last lines, she wrote, early in the evening. She was expecting her grandson soon. When he left, she would seal her confession and put it by her bedside. She would leave directions, where to find the will. Then she would take the bitter medicine, the final medicine, the stuff that would put her painlessly to sleep. And that would be that.

She ended with expressions of gratitude and love: to Tommy, with some words of advice I won't detail here, advice about getting job training, about hiring a financial manager, and more. She asked him to live a good life, and to honor her memory. She wanted him to put flowers on her grave on the anniversary of her death.

She also expressed gratitude and love to her dear nieces, Karen and Barbara, for all they had done for her. She wanted them to remember her with kindness. She was leaving this life without regrets.

Karen had been looking over my shoulder. And when she saw these words, she burst out: "And this is how I repaid her!" and dissolved into tears. I comforted her as best I could. I think I did a pretty poor job of it, but at least I tried.

25

Well, basically, the story is over. Between Peter Elver's and Karen's confessions, and Harriet's letter, there were no more loose ends. Oh, yes, Tommy: he was released shortly after these events. The police and D.A. were still suspicious, as they usually are, but they had nothing to go on. He was still in a bit of trouble—about his role in disposing of Fosco's body. But Nolan Thom made short work of this. And I do think the police decided—maybe reluctantly—that Tommy had nothing to do with the earlier crimes, those killings in Arizona, that he was more of a victim than a perpetrator.

That finished the criminal case. At that point, my own hard work began. Once all this nonsense was out of the way, I had to get down to business, handling the estate and shepherding it through the probate process. But this was now no problem. And, in the end, I made a nice bit of money. And why not? I did a competent, professional job. In the end, too, Joe Pangea got his legacy. Tommy, Barbara, and Karen got what Harriet had left them. The three of them became, to put it bluntly, seriously and permanently rich.

I don't know what Barbara and Karen will do with the money. They did go on a fancy cruise, the Greek Islands or something, but I imagine they'll be careful with their inheritance. Karen will spend some of it, no doubt, looking for and finding more and more lore about the magnificent Spively's. Maybe she'll write a book about this most illustrious family. Barbara laughs at this idea. "She'll find out some of the Spively's owned slaves or cheated in business, and then what'll she do?"

Barbara herself will be careful with the money. She won't fritter it away, I'm sure of that.

How Tommy will handle his money is another question. Now that he's a millionaire, I offered him my services; he needed what we call estate planning, and badly. We had one short conversation after he got out of jail. He seemed, for the moment, somewhat dazed. I tried to get him to talk about what happened. He said very little, but he backed up Harriet's account. "She shot the guy... I was there, in the house. She... she was awesome. Man, I couldn't believe it. Me, I couldn't have done it, for anything. I'm scared of guns. And she did it for me! She was, like I said, awesome. She was afraid of nothing and nobody. And she loved me. Nobody ever loved me before, nobody. But Harriet, she did."

I had to agree. Harriet Wingate had been awesome. And rich. As for Tommy, he did agree to come see me again, professionally. I want him to set up some sort of trust, an arrangement with professional management. I want him to be able to lean back and enjoy the money without any headaches. *And* be free from the likes of Sophie.

As for Sophie... well, she split, shortly after the events I described. She saw the handwriting on the wall. Of course, Tommy would be rich after all, but he would never share his wealth with Sophie. Not a penny. She knew that. She knew that all along, from the conversation she overheard, the conversation she was meant to overhear (and which she lied to me about). She left to avoid getting ditched. She had the gall to call and tell me she was going. She said "don't bother trying to find me." I would never have tried. Some people are best off lost. She seemed bitter about the whole business. Maybe she was sorry she had wasted her precious time on Tommy. I asked her if Tommy knew she was leaving. She said he'll know when he finds me gone.

"He was going to dump me," she said, "and I'm not going to let that airhead have the last word."

She was right about Tommy. He made a promise to Harriet Wingate. Tommy is a guy who keeps his word. It just takes him a little time, he needs to work up his courage.

He'll find somebody else, have no fear. Somebody told me later that he had a new relationship. He had rented a very nice new apartment, and some chick (as the saying goes) was now sharing the accommodations. I wonder whether Tommy found her or she found Tommy. I only hope this is somebody nice, somebody decent, not another Sophie, not a woman who somehow sniffed the sweet, sweet odor of money and acted accordingly.

Peter Elver is under arrest, and disbarment is a lead pipe cinch. Stealing money from clients? That's a real no-no. The bar association can be very severe with lawyers who steal. You can't even mix a client's money with your own, much less spend it. He might also go to prison. I should feel sorry for him. His life is a shambles. But even when he was sniveling in my office, I had trouble feeling any empathy. He brought it on himself.

Anyway, as I said, everything went back to normal: the estate ran smoothly and at the end there was that excellent fee. Celia's dream of a remodeled bathroom will come true, as soon as we find the right contractor. The process fills me with dread. All those issues (blue tile or green?) which have to be resolved. I'll survive. And we'll have a bright new skylit bathroom.

This story was, as you can see, not the usual story of mystery and murder. For one thing, there's no real hero. I don't really qualify, do I? After all, I didn't solve it. I didn't have a brainstorm or analyze clues. I had decided one key thing: that Harriet Wingate probably killed herself, once I knew she died of poisoning. What made me pause was the fact that she left no note, no explanation. I felt, this wouldn't be like her. And there were other puzzling facts. How could I know about the yellow folder?

So the solution just fell into my lap. Why not? Most crimes get solved that way. Sherlock Holmes is fiction, pure invention. Real life is different. Well, you know that already.

I'm back, then, in my usual rut. Back to my clients. Who, like all of us, live and then die. Most of them, to my great relief, die a natural death.

About the author

Lawrence Friedman is a professor of law at Stanford University. He teaches courses in American legal history and law and society. He is the author of *A History of American Law*, *Crime and Punishment in American History*, *The Human Rights Culture*, and *Total Justice*, among other works. He recently published *Dead Hands: A Social History of Wills, Trusts, and Inheritances*, a subject which is the backbone of Frank May's (fictional) practice.

Visit us at *www.qpbooks.com*.

www.ingramcontent.com/pod-product-compliance
Lightning Source LLC
Chambersburg PA
CBHW071202260626
47162CB00003B/1139